Gerald Dawe was born in Belfast in 1952
Orangefield Boys' School, the New Univer
University College Galway. He has received
his poetry, including, in 1984, the Macaula
Literature. He edited the original edition of *The Younger Irish Poets* (1982) and co-edited, with Edna Longley, *Across a Roaring Hill: The Protestant Imagination in Modern Ireland* (1985). A collection of his literary journalism, *How's the Poetry Going? Literary Politics and Ireland Today*, will be published in 1991. He is founder-editor of *Krino* and teaches at Trinity College Dublin.

Poetry collections by Gerald Dawe:

Sheltering Places (Blackstaff Press, 1978)
The Lundys Letter (Gallery Press, 1985)
Sunday School (Gallery Press, 1991)

The
NEW
YOUNGER
IRISH
POETS

edited by

Gerald Dawe

THE
BLACKSTAFF PRESS
BELFAST

Some of these poems have previously appeared in *Belfast Review*, *Firebird 4: New Writing from Britain and Ireland* (Penguin Books, 1985), *Fortnight*, *Gown Literary Supplement*, *Honest Ulsterman*, *Irish Times*, *Krino*, *Map-Makers' Colours* (Nu-age Editions, 1988), *North Dakota Quarterly*, *Poetry Ireland Review*, *Raven Introductions 6* (Raven Arts Press, 1990), *Salmon*, *Sunday Tribune*'s 'New Irish Writing', *Trio Poetry 6* (Blackstaff Press, 1990)

First edition published in 1982 by
The Blackstaff Press Limited
entitled *The Younger Irish Poets*

This fully revised and updated edition published in 1991 by
The Blackstaff Press Limited
3 Galway Park, Dundonald, Belfast BT16 0AN, Northern Ireland
with the assistance of
The Arts Council of Northern Ireland

Typeset by Textflow Services Limited
Printed by The Guernsey Press Company Limited
British Library Cataloguing in Publication Data
The New Younger Irish Poets.
1. Ireland. English poetry
I. Dawe, Gerald
821.91408
ISBN 0-85640-460-8

for
my two patronesses

The act of writing is itself political in the fullest sense. A good poem is a paradigm of good politics – of people talking to each other, with honest subtlety, at a profound level.

Derek Mahon, 1970

CONTENTS

Ireland is visibly a literary culture. Portraits and photographs of Irish writers festoon public bars, hotel lobbies, restaurants, and throughout the country plaques commemorate the residences of many writers. Indeed, poetry has a curious public life in Ireland that often gives a misleading notion of just how central it *actually* is in Irish society. In many of the poems which follow, the individual poet's own self-consciousness at being a poet is often similarly on display.

Cork-based Thomas McCarthy's poems question and document his sense of the poet as a true son of the Republic struggling to find an artistic poise that is not provincially self-limiting or culturally bland and complacent. John Hughes, however, takes much of this questioning for granted – in common with several other poets from the north of Ireland who grew up into the poetically charged literary environment of the 1980s. Hughes, Andrew Elliott, Kevin Smith and Patrick Ramsey – all from the north – have a remarkable, unpretentious confidence, a range of reference and a self-deprecating wit. They can often be thought of as cavaliers in the puritan culture of their own place. Or maybe it is the other way round, as Hughes remarks in his poem 'Puritans and cavaliers':

> When it's all but over I return to bed
> and phone you to arrange a lunchtime rendezvous
> in the grounds of the City Hall,
> for it's vital I understand once and for all
> how unnatural some of my practices are.
> What are the questions to be answered?
> Are you a puritan? Am I a cavalier?
> Breathless, I lie among a pile of your underclothes.

In a sense these poets from the north and south, east and west of Ireland write against the tide of moralising arguments, having heard through years of television, radio and newspaper reports, interviews, retrospectives and so forth, an endless and seemingly grand debate about the rights and wrongs of history. For when everyone has a point to make, claiming truth on their side – as the statistics of terror continue to mount and the possibility of change seems ever more remote – the poets here, particularly those from the north, display keen tactics of evasion. Their instincts, it seems to me, are for creative survival in a dearth of social and political movement, exposing hypocrisy rather than challenging it head-on.

And who would blame them? On the one hand, the northern poets have spent their teenage years and early twenties within a country locked in, what has best been called, by the playwright and novelist Thomas Kilroy, 'a struggle for the irretrievable'. Nostalgia and anger, under-standing and rejection, self-enfolding ennui and insider knowingness can so easily thwart the normally resilient and well-defined ambition of a young poet's artistic drive. On the other hand, the development and confidence of a number of women poets, especially those, such as Mairéad Byrne, who live in the south, and the more political engagements with that state manifested in the work of poets like Michael O'Loughlin or Dermot Bolger show how difficult it is to talk of a generation in Irish poetry with a common agenda.

Wry northern disillusion meets earnest southern commit-ment? Well, not quite. Each of the twenty-one poets has a distinct individual style – from the refined self-possession of Sara Berkeley to the ludicrous mockeries of John Kelly, from the comic teasing of Julie O'Callaghan, that carries a desper-ate poignancy as well, to the entrapments that Rita Ann Higgins's personae speak of in their barely suburban homes. At the same time poets like Dennis O'Driscoll, Aidan Carl Mathews, Sebastian Barry, Peter Sirr and Peter McDonald bring to their work an almost haughty seriousness and presumption that flies in the face of the gross caricatures of Irish poetry as an introverted, sour wrangling over cultural identity. And other voices, such as those of Martin Mooney, Pat Boran and Brendan Cleary, exhibit a fresh uncompro-mised intelligence which never becomes merely clever or glibly sophisticated.

What follows, then, is a selection of poems written in English by Irish poets born in the 1950s and 1960s. For developments in Irish-language poetry readers are referred to the definitive anthology, *An Tonn Gheal: The Bright Wave* (Raven Arts Press, 1986), edited by Dermot Bolger, which includes English translations by several poets featured in this book.

Only two contributors have been retained from *The Younger Irish Poets* (1982) – McCarthy and Mathews – whose poetry, along with that of O'Driscoll, O'Callaghan, Higgins, Barry and Seán Dunne, embodies a style appropriate to the general mood of this new anthology. They illustrate, within some sense of continuity, the shifting alignments of younger Irish poets within the divided country of Ireland, between Ireland, Britain and Europe (where several of them live), by the manner in which they attempt to create their own aesthetic response in the face of politics and history – no mean achievement given the brash and often mean-spirited state that was the 1980s.

Finally, I would particularly like to thank Blackstaff Press and Geraldine Mangan for all their work and help in bringing this anthology to print.

GERALD DAWE

GALWAY AND DUBLIN, 1991

THOMAS McCARTHY

b. 1954

STATE FUNERAL

Parnell will never come again, he said. He's there, all that was
mortal of him. Peace to his ashes.

James Joyce, Ulysses

That August afternoon the family
Gathered. There was a native *déjà vu*
Of Funeral when we settled against the couch
On our sunburnt knees. We gripped mugs of tea
Tightly and soaked the TV spectacle;
The boxed ritual in our living room.

My father recited prayers of memory,
Of monster meetings, blazing tar-barrels
Planted outside Free State homes, the Broy-
Harriers pushing through a crowd, Blueshirts;
And, after the war, de Valera's words
Making Churchill's imperial palette blur.

What I remember is one decade of darkness,
'A mind-stifling boredom; long summers
For blackberry picking and churning cream,
Winters for saving timber or setting lines
And snares: none of the joys of here and now
With its instant jam, instant heat and cream:

It was a landscape for old men. Today
They lowered the tallest one, tidied him
Away while his people watched quietly.
In the end he had retreated to the first dream,
Caning truth. I think of his austere grandeur;
Taut sadness, like old heroes he had imagined.

BREAKING GARDEN

He's reluctant to move; old campaigner
Familiar with siege. He had spent hours
On violent streets during the thirties,
Refusing to move despite batons and gas:
But this is the year of forced migration;
Letters, books are stuffed in bags like grain,
Pictures and paperweights, crumbling squadrons
Of files await the retreating campaign.

She's more resigned. Quiet in acquiescence:
She moves quickly between rows of growth,
Deciding which plants must stay. I watched her
For days. With two sheepdogs for lieutenants
She tested the tallest stems; made a note
Of the tough ones, those likely to endure.

RETURNING TO DE VALERA'S COTTAGE

Coming down the hill we could see the summer
village, millwheel and stream
churning up the wet sunlight.
The village seemed brighter
then without the dark weight
of his heavy cloak or a threat
of his sword-cane over their
votes. Their great child had been dead for years.

So that ordinary children came back onto the street
while adults gossiped lightly
unafraid of the official cars –
not that he was held in awe,
but the walking evidence of

2

so intense a life frightened
the whole village and kept them from serious thought.

In finding his cottage we found a life that was
inside ourselves. A small
moment of sorrow. A tear
riding down the glass of
our eyes like blood fall-
ing from a bullet wound.
We kicked the heap of weeds
with our heels and cursed the narrowness of the path.

HER WIDOWHOOD

Ba mhaith liom triall go deireadh lae go brónach.
Seán Ó Ríordáin

A shaft of wind cuts through the wet garden,
Daffodils are forced to their full shower
Of yellowness. The tall azara that smelled
Of chocolate has sprung to life once more
Though its bark was cut, its bole half sawn.
Something of the old regeneration has left
Me: birds seem quiet, the furrows less clear.
The accuracy of new growth that blessed
Love's wandering eyes at our first sowing
Seems non-existent in the huge quietness
Left by his death. Plants revolt in my head –
This widowhood is like a nettle sting,
Blotching one's whole body with its whiteness,
Filling limbs and seed with the ache of the dead.

THE PROVINCIAL WRITER'S DIARY

On cold nights in November he read late
and worried about the gift of fiction;
he was enveloped in a shell of lethargy.
Everything was let go –
even his diary lay idle for a whole month
while he chased provincial loneliness
from the corners of his mother's house.

Everything became consumed by the Personal:
furious theatre work killed some time,
strolling with his bachelor friends, fishing,
or the steady cumulative ritual of walking
beyond the city to sketch its grey limits.
But nowhere could he find (within those limits
of thought) the zeal that would consume life.

He lived far from the heroic. On Monday
mornings he would stalk the grey ghettos
of the North side and low-lying tenements
for absentee school children. He would be taken aback
by the oppressive stench and filth of their lives.
One morning he thought, as if explaining all misery,
that such homes were the nests of the Military.

THE PRESIDENT'S MEN

There's dust on Mr Dineen's boots! Where has
he been canvassing? I wonder. What house
has unlatched a half-day of harvest work
to listen to his talk? My father knows
the Party poll, the roll calls of promise;
the roads we shall take when I am older

4

in search of power. We'll find it like cress
on farms of green and vegetal water.

The sound of bagpipe music! Just listen!
From my father's shoulder I can see above
the crowd, Mr Dineen's careful parade,
men struggling to keep the roadway open,
sunlight in my father's hair, the glitter of
pipers' braids; the President's cavalcade.

QUESTION TIME

Question time at the end of another Election Year;
senators and their wives dancing on the ballroom floor;
children in corners dropping crisps and cream,
their fathers ordering them home, their mothers in
    crinoline
having to put them outside to sulk in the Christmas dark.
Enmities dissolving now in a sea of drink and smoke and
    talk.

Who was Robert Emmet's mistress? Who was Kitty
    O'Shea?
Which IRA man was shot on his own wedding day?
How many death warrants did Kevin O'Higgins sign?
So much to answer between the buffet meal and wine –
but the prize is a week in Brussels, money for two,
and kisses from two Euro-MPs just passing through.

WINDOWS

The windows of our flat: their shutters
disperse the worst fogs of the winter

so that I can see the quays falling
into the tidal mouth of the river –
since I moved as high as these windows
I've overheard the nightlife of ghosts:
British officers taking their boots off,
Cork whores dropping hints and slips,
their accents putting on airs. Also,
servants in the evening (the year 1901,
maybe) when all their chores were done
tiptoeing to their bedrooms. The horses
on Wellington Road are made of glass,
their liveried coachmen are throwing
wet oats at the windows of our flat.

THE STANDING TRAINS

. . . and I thought how wonderful to miss one's connections;
soon I shall miss them all the time
                              Louis MacNeice, *The Strings are False*

From the windows of a standing train
you can judge the artwork of our poor Republic.
The prominent ruins that make Limerick Junction
seem like Dresden in 1945
and the beaten-up coaches at Mallow Station,
the rusted sidetracks at Charleville,
have taken years of independent thought.
It takes decades to destroy a system
of stations. On the other hand, a few
well-placed hand signals can destroy a whole
mode of life, a network of happiness.
This is our own Republic! O Memory,
O Patria, the shame of silenced junctions.
Time knew we'd rip the rails apart, we'd sell
emigrant tickets even while stripping

the ticket office bare. The standing trains
of the future were backed against a wall.

Two hens peck seed from the bright platform,
hens roost in the signal box.
Bilingual signs that caused a debate in the Senate
have been unbolted and used as gates:
it's late summer now in this dead station.
When I was twelve they unbolted the rails.
Now there's only the ghost of my father,
standing by the parcel shed with his ghostly
suitcase. When he sees me walking towards him
he becomes upset. *Don't stop here!* he cries.
Keep going, keep going! This place is dead.

SHROUD

Electorates, not politicians, disappear without trace,
television our perfectly mortal linen.
The Taoiseach's face comes into grey focus
like the lately usurped Turin Shroud.
His speech is barely audible;
the early-morning crowd
jostles against the thirsting press corps.
Flashbulbs tell
us what we already know:
he is tired, probably ill, becoming scared.
The helicopter gun ships of the political campaign
have left unbearable ringing in our ears,
and cynical decompression.
What is it that keeps the politicians going?
Is it like the Shroud itself, a Jesus thing –
that some woman might touch the hem of his Government

7

and become a comforted mother, lover, or some dark
  Magdalene
wipe perspiration from his face, the years
of wilderness, to leave an immortal imprint?

DENNIS O'DRISCOLL

b. 1954

FLATLAND

Takeaway foods, small late-night stores,
record dealers, posters for Folk Mass.
Coke and Kentucky Fried Chicken make an ideal meal
  here,
unpacked in a bedsitter and swallowed near a one-bar fire.

Down bicycle-cluttered corridor, by coinbox telephone,
special-offer leaflets, buff uncollected post,
weekends open optimistically beforehand
like sands of package-holiday brochures.

Falling plaster bares timber ceiling ribs,
like piano keys stripped of their ivory; fireplaces are
  blocked.
Revolving record wheels, slow music after pubs,
will transport lovers into a seagull-velvet dawn,

into stale cigarette smoke, lingering tastes of beer;
outside, ivy-bearded trees shelter the rubbish bins;
milk cartons roll, great lice, through long-haired lawns;
the hall door buttoned with bells.

In neat gardens on the next street, wickerwork branches
will be baskets full with fruit yet.
Couples yawn and part. Sunday now,
the heavy hours weigh down the scales of watch

to four o'clock, sports programmes on the radio,
as evening's cigarette butt is stubbed out,
leaving an ash-grey sky
which only a working Monday will illuminate.

PORLOCK

this is the best poem I have never written
it is composed of all the stunning lines I thought of
but lacked the time or place or paper to jot down

this is a poem of distractions, interruptions, clamouring
    telephones
this is a poem that reveals how incompatible with verse my
    life is
this is a home for mentally handicapped poems

this is the lost property office of poetry
this is my poem without a hero, conceived but never born
this is a prisoner of consciousness, a victim of intelligence
    leaks

this is the poem that cannot learn itself by heart
this is the poem that has not found its individual voice
this is the poem that has forgotten its own name

this is my most unmemorable creation
these are my most disposable lines
this is the poem that dispenses with words

WINGS

like tumbling masonry pigeons drop from a building
magpies flock for gold to where sun inscribes a tree

the heron paddles with its skirts rolled up
lapwings at their air base wear a crew cut

thrushes pluck a field's loose threads
kettle swans simmer on electric rings

a team of wild geese rows across the evening cheering
and an exhibitionist bat opens a mackintosh

the hawk plays darts, the swallows skate
the drunken cuckoo hiccups one last time

then night's television screen of stars is switched on
a murder story with the owl's loud screams

REPUBLICAN SYMPATHIES

*What I have always liked about the Irish Republic is that it is,
of all the societies that I know, the least 'sexy'.*
                                                                Donald Davie

It is always raining on this bleak country.
Windows in their rustproof frames are never silent.
Our cottages are damp-proofed to no avail.
Bruise marks of mould deface wallpaper skin.
Smells of decay assail us in our musty sitting rooms.

How could sexiness survive this purifying climate?
Where would cutaway shoes, see-through blouses,
figure-hugging mini skirts fit into this arthritic scheme?
Chunky-knits and padded anoraks are the order of the day;
hot-water bottles, flannel bedwear make nights sensuous.

Somewhere, annually, Miss Ireland is announced
and shivers in ciré swimwear just long enough
for ogling lenses to record her nerve.
Occasionally, too, fishnets and high heels are glimpsed,
springing across a bus-stop flood . . .

Forecasts are seldom good here, bringing forebodings
of worse weather, deteriorating trade, added
    unemployment.

Days are so dark the end of the world never appears far
    off.
Hay floats, unharvested, in flooded fields.
The beauty of this land lies mostly in reflection.

Our birth rate stays high (boredom? Vatican encyclicals?):
erotic signals are given off, it seems – muffled
behind layers of ribbed woollen tights, thermal underwear.
What need have we of sex shops, contraceptives?
Yielding Sheela-na-Gigs are cut down to size by an east
    wind;

summer is a few golden straws to grasp on between
    showers.

HOME AFFAIRS

I

Death is moving into newly constructed suburbs,
through semi-detached houses, ugly identical twins.
Hired cars will call for widows who had come as brides . . .

Where readymix cement ejects from giant hair driers,
the foundations of our married lives are laid.
We will slice the keyhole loaf of bread together here.

This evening, a rainbow unfolded its colour chart
and I imagined these dwellings once painted, tamed:
the knock of radiators in a dry-lined sitting room;

whispers and bickerings filtered through air vents;
the small-hour lulls only the troubled sleepers know
or babysitters waiting for the owners to reach home.

II

Dashed house fronts gleam like popcorn, a mirage
seen from what will be the main road through estates,
bearing working couples, coal deliveries or crowded bus,
pavements reserved for tricycles, shopping trolleys, prams.

We are strolling on its asphalt arc, a desert airstrip
covering ancient cow tracks, smoothing paths,
a digger's tyre marks – arrowheads – along its verge.
All we will reap from now on in this raw settlement

are plastic piping, gypsum board and brick.
Our new fridges and washing machines will rust
in mountains of our indestructible sediment,
our baths end up as drinking troughs.

In the distempered house, we try to appear civilised,
use silvery bins, hang prints, keep carpets swept,
at evening listen to symphonies, or read,
hearing container trucks along the dual carriageway.

With a poker for sword, a fireguard for shield,
you provoke the blazing fangs to fume and spit.
Will they know peace who sit quietly in their own rooms?
I trace the Braille goosebumps of your body

and begin to lip-read as the night intensifies.

III

It is an ordinary morning without pain.
Sun's spotlight stares from a dishevelled sky,
ruffled with clouds like a safety curtain.
Summer is in heat again: gooseberry scrotums swell,
hard blackberry knuckles will soon ooze with blood.

The window swings out onto a butterfly-light breeze,
a heady aura of sweet peas, rose fumes, poppy seasoning.
Cut lawns exude fresh hay; grasshopper blades whirr;
resinous smells of wood pervade the tool shed.
No bad news breaks today, no sudden tragedy, no urgent
   telegrams,

no hospital visiting, no pacing outside intensive care units.
The sun blossoms in its foliage of cloud
and we fortify ourselves with its light, our house's silence,
against the trouble, bustle, pain
which other mornings will, irrevocably, bring.

A LAMENT FOR WILLY LOMAN

There was a sadness about him always.
Even as he beamed another of his hopes
some darkness would eclipse his smile,
creeping along each hemisphere of his face.
But he looked so good in a pressed suit
heading off to some place in New England,
smelling of shaving cream, hair oil, soap,
cuff links and tiepin glinting like a candidate's.
Or like one of the Chevy's hubcaps
that I'd rub and rub until its fish-eye
would brim with his grinning reflection.

I wonder where the car – red it was – is now.
Its smell, too, stays with me: of new seats,
roof upholstery, lacquered dash,
whetting memory like that store downtown
where Pop bought flower plants, seeds
and we prepared the mud, uprooting tentacles of weed.
Sun no longer takes in that part of the yard,
too many buildings sprouted where we played.

14

Those years Pop seemed brave and strong
as we waved him off to conquer territories.
Now he grows small and sweats with terror
in my sleep and I can hardly picture how he was.
If he were still around, we'd probably be feuding . . .
Yet I'd love to bring him for a proper meal
and talk and fill his mouth with all
the things I denied him in his life.

Maybe he has entered his happy phase
– dreams realised, quotas reached.
I remember him on nights in our hot kitchen
totting his commission up, the radio's babble
like a nagging worry in the background.
People said I looked like Pop and when he died
I inherited his inconsolable eyes.
Something like a brake screeched in me
as he drove off to meet with death.

Waiting for the autopsy to end, I thought
of how he'd said: 'When I am President,
first thing I'll do is to ban artificial flowers.'
So it was fresh roses Mom took to his grave.

REMEMBERING MARINA TSVETAYEVA

Hair straight as a witch's, face foretelling its future,
you walked these Paris streets with your dumpy son.
(Did you starve yourself to keep him fed?)
But I still prized our months of ecstasy in Prague,
the silken skin surviving under a threadbare shift,
your green eyes shining out of the darkness
where you prowled – slim and frisky as a cat –
our passion squeezed through every pore.

You were wild and volatile, an endangered species,
yielding your quivering pelt on the mountain floor.
I can hardly look your poems in the eye these days,
they hang our old emotions out like underclothes.
The Julian calendar's certainties had been abolished,
Crimean afternoons around the stewing samovar
– you used declaim your verses then, weave your spell
Godlike as a spider in its web of entrapped flies.

The trials of repatriation summoned years ahead:
your husband would be shot, your daughter detained;
the rope you'd knot your life with would be spun.
Your story is a film the audience leaves early.
They know how it will end, there will be no surprises,
no reprieve, happiness never the twist your fate secretes.
What you'll learn is that the body you create and cook with
must be lumbered from sticky sick bed to prison gates;

that love goes unrequited; that children outgrow parents;
that blows, like poems, come in cycles; that truth
    persecutes.
Do not return to Moscow, Marina. Do not return.
Petals drip from my cherry tree, casting an arc
of blossoms, a pink splash animating spring grass
that makes me wish we could link arms again
and, among these shuttered boulevards, exchange our
    plans
with the surreptitious fervour of lovers or of spies.

THE CONFORMIST VILLAGE

Loving your work represents the best, most concrete
approximation of happiness on earth.
Primo Levi

We are marching for work:
people fresh from dream bedrooms,
people whose flesh begins to slip
like old linoleum loosening on a floor,
people with head colds and love bites,
girls startlingly immaculate,
pores probed with cleanser,
ribboned hair still wet,
giving off a shampooed scent;

people taking their tastes and troubles
to the conformist village of the office
where everyone sets about the routine tasks,
their identities subsumed
into the uniform regimen of work.
We forego initiative and drive
for the security of such places,
a foyer guard by the spotlit tapestry;
soft furnishings; a constant heat.

'
We are wasting our lives
earning a living, underwriting new life,
grateful at a time of unemployment
to have jobs, hating what we do.
Work is the nightmare we yearn to wake from,
the slow hours between tea breaks
spent vetting claims, scanning VDUs.
We are the people at the other end
of telephone extensions when you ring,

the ones who put a good face on the firm,
responding to enquiries, parrying complaints,
the ones without the luck to have inherited
long-laned retreats, fixed-income bonds,
who yield to lunchtime temptations,
buy clothes and gadgets, keep retail spending high.
The half-lit office buildings – white squares, black –
that we turn our backs on after overtime
are crosswords we must pass the years with,

filling to distraction our blank days.

JULIE O'CALLAGHAN

b. 1954

DAYS

I used to spend my days
strumming a *koto*,
arranging fresh blossoms
in a painted vase,
reciting the poem that begins
'The days and months flow by'
or, with a brush, painting the view.
But my parents
wanted me to go to court
and find a husband.
So, now I live
with the other ladies-in-waiting
and never have
a moment to myself.

THREE PAINTINGS BY EDWARD HOPPER

I
Chop Suey

'Isn't it fun to come down here
away from the kids
and eat in Chinatown
during winter?
After fiddling with our chopsticks
and drinking tea from those funny little cups,
we'll take the bus
to Saks Fifth Avenue or Bergdorf Goodman's
and try on expensive clothes.'

'Look out the window
at the restaurant sign –
all you can see is "Suey" –
the "Chop" must be further up.'

II
Nighthawks

The heat and the dark
drive us from apartments
down empty streets
to the all-night diner
where fluorescent lights
illuminate us like tropical fish
in a fish tank.
We sit side by side
listening to glasses clank,
the waiter whistling,
and stare at the concrete outside.
Not looking at our watches
or counting the cigarettes
and cups of coffee.

III
Automat

I thought when I came here
I'd get rich as a secretary
and marry my boss.
I dreamt about that so long
I thought it would happen.
Maybe I should go back.

I hate small places though
and when I sit eating at the automat
I pretend I'm a celebrity
and all those walls of plastic doors
are really crowds of camera lenses
waiting to take my picture.

THE OBJECT

Hold me only when necessary.
Put me back newly dusted off
and in the proper place.
Look at me from the correct distance
at the few moments every day
when the sun filters through the room,
striking me at an advantageous angle.

Please try not to upset
my delicate composition.
Don't be tempted to change my position,
or demand more
than that I am here,
in the right lighting,
looking as best I can.

TEA BREAK

The Queen deserves to be rich,
she works harder than us.
I was never so bored as by Chekhov.
You don't like anything.
I think capital punishment should be brought back.
What are you doing this weekend.
Did you watch that show on TV last night.
I'm reading *The Carpetbaggers*,
it's filthy but very good.
Don't they make a lovely couple.
I'm buying shoes at lunchtime.
The girl making tea has a tattoo on her arm.
How much would you say she earns.
I'm so fed up.

My driving lesson's on Saturday.
Who's doing the collection.
Do you like that new song.
We have the best educational system in the world.
I'd never leave Ireland.
I saw this gorgeous dress.
My mother always says.
I've got a headache.
She makes me so angry.
How do you know.
That's just your opinion.

THE LITTLE GIRL

The scratchy couch at my grandmother's
creaked as she pointed to a little girl
in a class photograph.
'And who's this?'
I brought the album
close to my face to decide.
All my brain would tell me was
'It's you, of course,
don't you even know yourself
when you see yourself?'
'It's me,' I said,
although I couldn't remember
any of the girls or the dress.
'Look again,' she said.

WHAT I SAW

The man who lives on the left side of us
just tiptoed through our back yard

carrying a stick with a pair of pantyhose
waving on the top like a banner.
He climbed into the back yard of the people
who live on our right and lowered
the unmentionables onto the clothesline,
then hopped back over two fences
and was gone.

MARKETING

'Tell me honestly, now,
'cause it's your age bracket
we're aiming at:
what do ya think?
It's a bucket, a plastic bucket.
You could put a plant in it,
fill it with water
and buy a goldfish,
bring it to the store
and put your groceries in it,
if you're into cleanliness
you could use it to mop the floor,
you can turn it upside down
and sit on it or use it as a table.
See, it's a product for
the alternative generation.
We're getting them printed up
with "The Fuck-it Bucket" in bright letters.
You'll have the choice of
a marijuana plant,
horoscope calendar, the peace sign
or a rainbow underneath the letters.
It's a symbol, it says,
"We've had it with your bourgeois containers,

this is what we're for:
a working-class bucket." '
He straightened his twenty-dollar tie,
took a sip from his martini
and gazed down at the street twenty-eight storeys below.
'It'll be bigger than the hula-hoop.'

A TOURIST COMMENTS ON THE LAND OF HIS
    FOREFATHERS

Take Dublin for instance:
what is it anyway?
You walk across O'Connell Bridge,
little kids begging – gives the place atmosphere;
ya look around through a flea-bitten crowd
and wonder why they stay here.
Their cousins in Milwaukee write,
saying *come on over – we'll fix ya up*.
But no, it's safer going to ceilis and mass,
please God-ing and making themselves believe that
Grafton Street is elegant and an ice-cream cone
in summer is high adventure.

As for me, I got some great shots of the place
and as soon as I get back to the U S of A
I'll put them right where they belong:
first in the projector shining on our living-room wall
and then in a bright yellow Kodak box
next to all the others in my sock drawer.
No offence meant.

Mel
– Yeah
Quit watching that baseball game
– Pipe down and get me a Budweiser
Mel
– Whadya want
Let's go see a movie er somethin'
– Nay, this next guy might hit a grand slam
Mel
– Go with Shirley er Audrey
I wanna go with my husband
– My god, right the hell outta the ball park
Mel
– Knock it off
I wish WGN would go out of business
– Fat chance blabber mouth

Daddy, I know lots of neat songs.
– Really? Sing me one.
OK. 'Let's get physical, physical. I wanna get . . .'
– Know any others?
Yeah. 'She's a man-eater, watch out boys . . .'
– Where'd you learn those?
You play them on the phonograph.
– You've got a good memory for a five year old.
'Lemme hear your body talk, your body talk.'
– Did you ever sing them for Mommy?
Sure. 'Watch out boys she'll eat you up.'
– What did she think?
She said I could go with her to the beauty parlor.
– Why d'ya wanna go there?
So nobody'll reco'nise me after vacation.
– Sing me some more.

Um, excuse me an' everything
but did you two sleep OK last night?
Ya see neither of us got a wink.
That lady said that the bed we'd have
was like a Queen size and what it really was
was a three-quarter, right Fred?
Fred and me are used to a Queen size.
We had one ever since our honeymoon.
Can you imagine us in a three-quarter?
Maybe here in Ireland a three-quarter is a Queen size –
but not in the States, I-can-tell-you!
Gee, we could hardly breathe.
You've gotta really cute country
only Fred and I'd be better off at home
if a three-quarter is a Queen size.
We'd be too tired to see it.

Grandma, whisper, everybody's turning around.
– Well is she being thrown out of the convent?
No, she's just going to be a governess for a while.
– What does she have on?
A brown dress, hat and she's carrying a suitcase.
– Where's she going, is she walking or what?
Yeah, she's walking to the house where she's going to
    work.
– Why didn't they pick her up in a carriage?
So she could sing a song on the way.
– Is this a true story?
I guess so.
– Well I bet they picked her up.
Now she's meeting the family.
– She marries the father, Ingrid told me.
He's very handsome and rich.
– I thought you said she was still a nun . . .

It won't be tonight.
– I don't reckon why it shouldn't be.
I know it, feel it in my bones.
– I don't see how you're so gol-darned positive.
Everything is against it, don't you see?
– Nope, 'fraid I don't.
My god, look at the moon, listen to the crickets.
– What've the moon and crickets to do with it?
It's just all wrong, nothing like that could happen tonight.
– Well, we'll just see about that I s'pose.
It's too peaceful and quiet to come tonight.
– Welp it's gotta happen soon, anyhow.
Yes, of course, very soon, only – what was that?
– Some kind of screaming it sounded like.
Maybe we only imagined it, we're so tired waiting.
– My ears heard a scream and I aim to find out why.

THE GREAT BLASKET ISLAND

Six men born on this island
have come back after twenty-one years.
They climb up the overgrown roads
to their family houses
and come out shaking their heads.
The roofs have fallen in
and birds have nested in the rafters.
All the whitewashed rooms
all the nagging and praying
and scolding and giggling
and crying and gossiping
are scattered in the memories of these men.
One says, 'Ten of us, blown to the winds –
some in England, some in America, some in Dublin.
Our whole way of life – extinct.'

27

He blinks back the tears
and looks out across the island
past the ruined houses, the cliffs
and out to the horizon.

Listen, mister, most of us cry sooner or later
over a Great Blasket Island of our own.

RITA ANN HIGGINS

b. 1955

SECRETS

Secrets are for keeping
not for hiding,
the spines of wardrobes
will talk, sooner or later.

Keep your secrets in your heart,
in hip joints,
between folds of flesh,
or under rotting ulcers.

Never tell best friends,
in time their minds will leak
from old age or too much whiskey.

Don't succumb to pleas of
'I swear I'll never tell',
eleven will know within the hour.

Don't ever tell priests.

Keep well clear of burning bushes,
investigative mothers-in-law
with eggshell slippers
and Dundee cake.

Never tell the living dead.

Be on the lookout
for lean neighbours
who slither between hedges
and pose as ant-eaters.

They're really secret stealers in disguise.

As for keeping a diary,
when you're gone,
for entertainment, on wet days

and after funerals,
your nearest and dearest
will read it aloud with relish.

Try blushing with clay between your teeth.

SUNNY SIDE PLUCKED

We met outside
the seconds chicken
van at the market.

He was very American,
I was very married.

We chatted about
the home-made marmalade
I bought two miles
from home.

He said the eggs were big,
I said he'd been eating
his carrots.

'Do you always buy
seconds chickens?'

'Only when I come late.'

The witch in me
wanted to scramble
his eggs.

The devil in him
wanted to pluck
my chicken.

We parted
with an agreement
written by the eyes.

SOME PEOPLE

for Eoin

Some people know what it is like

to be called a cunt in front of their children
to be short for the rent
to be short for the light
to be short for school books
to wait in Community Welfare waiting rooms full of smoke
to wait two years to have a tooth looked at
to wait another two years to have a tooth out (the same
    tooth)
to be half strangled by your varicose veins, but you're
    198th on the list
to talk into a banana on a jobsearch scheme
to talk into a banana on a jobsearch dream
to be out of work
to be out of money
to be out of fashion
to be out of friends
to be in for the Vincent de Paul man

to be in space for the milkman
(sorry, Mammy isn't in today, she's gone to Mars for the
    weekend)
to be in Puerto Rico this week for the blanket man
to be in Puerto Rico next week for the blanket man
to be dead for the coalman
(sorry, Mammy passed away in her sleep, overdose of coal
    in the teapot)
to be in hospital unconscious for the rent man (St Jude's
    ward, 4th floor)
to be second hand
to be second class
to be no class
to be looked down on
to be walked on
to be pissed on
to be shat on

and other people don't.

WITCH IN THE BUSHES

for Padraic Fiacc

I know a man
who tried
to eat a rock,
a big rock
grey and hard,
unfriendly too.

Days later
he is still grinding,
the rock
is not getting
any smaller.

Because of this
rock in the jaw,
this impediment,
the man has become
even more angry.

No one
could look at him,
but a few
hard cases did.
They were mostly dockers;
they reckoned,

'We have seen
the savage seas
rise over our dreams,
we can look
at a bullhead
eating a rock.'

The years passed
slowly and painfully,
until one day
the rock was no more,
neither was much of the man.

He didn't
grind the rock down,
the rock
hammered a job
on him and his ego.

Then, one day
an old woman
came out of the bushes
wearing a black patch

and a questionnaire,
in her wand hand
she held a posh red pencil,
well pared.

She questioned him
between wheezes
(she had emphysema
from smoking damp tobacco
and inhaling fumes
from her open fire
in the woods)
if all that anger
for all those years
was worth it.

Old Rockie Jaw
couldn't answer,
he had forgotten
the reason
and the cause.

He concluded,
'Anger is OK
if you spill it,
but chewing
is assuredly
murder on the teeth.'

He had learned
his lesson,
he would
pull himself together,
smarten up like,
turn the other cheek,

he would go easy
on the oils that aged him.

Every now and then
he weakened,
he let the voice
from the rock take over,
an army voice
with a militant tone,

'A man is a man
and a real man
must spit feathers
when the occasion arises.'

Like all good voices
this one
had an uncle,
it was the voice
of the uncle
that bothered him,
it always
had the same warning,

'About
the witch in the bushes,'
it said,
'watch her,
she never sleeps.'

IT WASN'T THE FATHER'S FAULT

His father
hit him
with a baseball bat

and he was
never right since.

Some say
he was never right
anyway.

Standing
behind the kitchen table
one Sunday before Mass
his mother said,

'If Birdie Geary
hadn't brought
that cursed baseball bat
over from America,

none of this would have happened.'

DAUGHTER OF THE FALLS ROAD

*In memory of Mairéad Farrell, murdered in Gibraltar, by SAS,
6 March 1988*

And the world heard
about the awfulness of it
and it got into
the minds of the people.

And it was bigger than them
and they feared it,
they feared the bullet
and the bomb,
but mostly their own thoughts.

And in the minds of some people
were thoughts of pity
for the mothers of the three,
thoughts of anger
about the bullets to their heads,
and fear for their own flesh and blood.

And people wondered
why they were there,
and what strength of thought
propelled them, what conviction.

Some said,
tell me now
the politics of the dead,
some mentioned the struggle,
and others said,
the sun shines, we see no war,
but the Irish rarely
feel the sun;
they've heard about the war.

And from the eyes of her brothers
tumbled acid tears,
passing the place of their heart,
seeping into closed fists,
and there was an acid tear ocean there
doing nothing. Waiting.

And in the minds of some people
came her mother and father,
they waited ten years,
now ten lifetimes won't bring her back.
Dead daughter of the Falls Road.

And there was talk
she had a boyfriend
who was tall,
whose acid tears tumbled
passing the place of his heart,
seeping into closed fists,
and there was an acid tear ocean there
doing nothing. Waiting.

And in the minds of a lot of people
was the Irish girl
and her two companions,
brought home in boxes
made from Spanish trees.

And the living don't think
in tall straight lines
and Birch means little
when you're breathing
and in the hearts of some people
came another great wave.

And a lot now hate the Spanish trees
and the great hard Rock,
the pitiless Rock,
stealer of Irish youth.

LIGHT OF THE MOON

Question:
Can you tell me
the way to the maternity?

Answer:
Walk on a beach

in the west of Ireland
at four in the morning
in the middle of summer
with a man who's six foot two
and you'll get there
sooner or later.

Question:
Is his height the problem?

Answer:
No, the problem rises
when you stop
to look at the moon.

Question:
So is the moon
the problem?

Answer:
No, not the moon itself
but the glare from the moon
which makes you say
in seagull Russian,

'Fuse me bix foot skew
in your stocking wheat
bould you kind werribly
if I jay on the bat of my flack
for the bext three quarters of a bour
the boon is milling me.'

Question:
And that's the answer?

Answer:
No, that's the question,
when he lies on top of you
for the next three quarters of an hour
shielding you from the light of the moon
the answer comes to you.

Question:
Like a flash?

Answer:
No, like the thundering tide.

LIMITS

There were limits
to what he could take
so he took limits,
sometimes he went
over the limits.

Othertimes the limits
went over him,
not in any aggressive way,
down the neck way
oil the oesophagus way.

Cool and refreshing
on a hot-summer's-day way,
so he had a problem
he had to watch it.

His mother said it
so did his wife, watch it
the wise ones said, watch it.

But sometimes
when he wasn't looking
limits got him
handcuffed him
forced him into it,
down the neck way
oil the oesophagus way.

When he was
over the limits
nobody wanted him,

he was
an unwashed, unwanted
unwilling, unattractive
over-the-limits slob.

Never give a job
to a slob Bob,
never give a bob
to a slob.

He never got wise
he only got older
the limits got higher
the climb got harder.

He reached nowhere
in gigtime,
anywhere in notime
he had no limits
no fun, no jokes
no-how, no jumpers.

Only sitters
who sat around with him
and blamed the grass for growing
the Government
the IRA
the ABC
the IUD
the UFO
the ITV
he was a paid-up member
of the sitters-and-blamers gang.

After a while
he had no need
to watch it,

limits now looked
for plump ones
half his measure
who still had fight.

He had fought
all his battles
and lost
he was a lost limit
a limitless loss,

a winner only
when his pockets
were full
and his jokes were new.

Who was he now
at thirty-five?
An unlimited old man
who hadn't lived

lingering on street corners
searching for
shoot-the-breeze friendships
without commitments
or frontiers.

SEBASTIAN BARRY

b. 1955

HERMAPHRODITUS
atque in perpetuum, frater, ave atque vale

Surprised by night she plays young brother
in jacket and bow. Her brief hair confuses.

Tables are put where the oak grows,
between them she walks in the late air.

The Ball ends two years of polite distrust.
To mark it, a friend with his evening's wine

falls at our feet, and a girl that passes
smiles at the boy in her voice. She

wishes to sit, and I lift her up
where a branch of the oak droops down

till her legs hang warm from the black bark.
Our play is elaborate, we never kiss. But

does she think it a fabrication? The days
dwindle quietly. She returns to England.

SUMMER DESK

Leave the desk for the rustling evening,
hurry to the dark trout river
through warm wood and dying bees.

Flowers on this rich-timbered top
in baked-earth bowls regret the day.
Abandon here the waiting page

and night can curl the rising leaf.
No more, Propertius, about Vertumnus,
old with his dust and roses.

AT A GATE OF ST STEPHEN'S GREEN

The same street crawls to its bridge, hurries
from the iron of this gate, grey-souled
despite attentions of each year.

A lane there keeps cars' breath, rough
tar, rough books, no metamorphic ease,
a school unknown to hummingbirds, giraffes.

Shoulders tired on a stair, always
to balconies, thin dying air, dark
sharp rooms to blade once earth-brown eyes.

Inconsolable evenings then
covered themselves in dwindled green.

Gardeners thud here dead-wood clay.
Around them, hours in unmarked graves.
A tree-root moves, or a damp mole.

FANNY HAWKE GOES TO THE MAINLAND FOREVER

Ashblue porcelain, straw dolls, child's rocking chair,
neat farms, boxwood beards, gilded sheaves for prayer,
Fanny Hawke of Sherkin Island, Quaker,
leaving her boundary stones to marry
a Catholic lithographer in Cork City,
no one on the new pier to wave her away,
neither an Easter visit nor Market Day.
Only the hindview of a sleepy fox, its brush

shoving like a sheaf of sense through bushes.
Goodbye to the baskets in a judged heap
in an angle of the breakfast room,
the sun ignoring the Atlantic and leaping
alone into the midst of her family,
rustle, starch, and grave methods,
to that good hypocrisy, goodbye.
Goodbye little brother with your long face.

Small smooth shells on the great strands
come with her on her fingers as nails.
She smells the lobster the boatmen found
in the ghostly sea when she herself was asleep,
waiting while she dreamt for this morning,
something spangled and strewn on the lightly
grassed dunes, something tart in the air
while she walked, banging her skirts.

Come, little Fanny Hawke, into the bosom
of us hard Catholics, be an outlaw for us.
Bring what you own in a seabox on
a true voyage like anything worth while,
your linens with simplest stitchings,
your evening head-cloths, your confident

plainness. Be sure that you bring all fresh
despite that they have cast you completely

onto the desert and mainland of your love.
Up the century, Fanny, with you, never mind.
Look at your elegant son, an improved Catholic
squaring up landscapes in his future
to paint them as they are, like a Quaker.
There is your other son, a scholarship painter,
a captain in a war, asthmatic, dying young,
all happening even as you set out, oh Fanny.

LINES DISCOVERED UNDER THE FOUNDATIONS OF
   DUBLIN IN A LANGUAGE NEITHER IRISH NOR ENGLISH

after a medieval Latin song

These our winter quarters may
be heavyhanded under rain,
the shelters morninglike with grogblossom,

but we choose still
to stay on longer here
and spurn the citizens

who walk to give us walls.
O teenage men waking
to moony pleasure, throw

your perhaps ungrateful
words among our imaginary
stockades and make

your fathers witty
in case these townsmen
with charters and wardens manage

to bloom their kingship
in our babble and rubbish.
On disappearing

timber, tell our Echo
Mountain, not expecting
your maydays to boom back. O

berry men, aim to plumb
every available custom.
We can bear most error

for the sacred racket
of each of you roaring
to his melancholy

brother, 'Keep the filthy
fathers inarticulate.
Keep nicks, companion!'

TROOPER O'HARA AT THE INDIAN WARS

My horse's head jangles on his martingale,
his spirit the same as this drenched May morning
with jewels of dew under the eucalyptus leaves
that rain on the ragworts, pearl before such swine.
My saddle is home
with a tuft of leather for my left hand
as our blue-coats brush through the mid-morning
and the red dust peppers the lather
and we are out among the Indian Wars.

Mulberries made the midnight of my hair,
my mother said,
which she knew from her berry gathering
to make her wine,
red, blue, goose, elder and sloe,
the lives of the blackthorn, my daddy's staff
in the cornmarket
through bins of the fading fool's gold of our farms
and the butter wharfs,
the sunk gold laced with salt to go to England.
My mother with her feet of many colours
after treading the oaken buckets
I think of, in the whey of here.

Yesterday, today, tomorrow
we kill wild native bowmen
savager surely than the English found us,
I hope, or this is fratricide.
We burn out the girls in the tumbleweeds and brush
who lie quiet as turtles,
as soft as does of hares,
brothel and butcher shop.

AIDAN CARL MATHEWS

b. 1956

LETTER FOLLOWING

We promise letters and send postcards,
My father and I. The whole of Europe
Has passed between us without comment

Down through the years, but mostly sailboats,
Waterfronts, and the polaroid heavens
Reflecting the sea or being reflected.

Only this morning, he sent me
The *Victory* in dry dock and 3-D,
Second time round. There's the usual

Men's talk about storms and maintenance:
When it worsened, then I worried would she
Drag her moorings, but she rode it well,

Her hatches battened. Is he talking
Marriages or jobs? Or a cabin cruiser
Idling at anchor, five sons and no crew?

Who can tell? Mid-afternoon,
I write him at his hospital
A card addressed to the Ancient Mariner,

Of an island ferry from six months back,
Its lifeboat circled and arrowed:
The best place to be in a headwind.

And I post it off from this dusty place,
Thirty miles inland, north of Salonica,
Among chickens and children. Word of thanks,

Word of greeting. This is our way.
We cover our multitudes, he and I,
Our silences carrying over the water.

ELEGY FOR A FIVE YEAR OLD

Bewildered tonight, how often
I lose and catch you as if
We two were at hide-and-seek
Round the house before lights-out.
Your mother is trying to speak.
Her mouth means it is I

Who must find you in bed,
Not moving, holding your breath.
You'll get your death of cold.
How can you know the trouble
You've caused, a hue and cry,
Vigil of phone calls, candles?

And who am I to explain
You have slipped off without warning
To be by yourself, or to say
'There is no point in our waking
All night at the least noise
Of footsteps over the gravel?

FOR SIMON, AT THREE AND FIVE

Two years ago, you brought me
A crayon drawing of a red cottage.
Pink sheep were at peace there.
The smoke went straight as a ruler

Between the sun and the moon
To a star cut from kitchenfoil.
That, you said, was the *most hardest*.

Today, I must learn to hang below it
A castle among tree stumps –
So they can't creep up on you –
And land mines under the vegetables.
That matchstick man in the staked pit
Twitches within an inch of his life:
His tears like a tap-drip

Drop and puddle in pearshapes,
Making a river that nudges round
The four corners of the sheet
To where another matchstick man
Is fishing without a care in the world,
His eyes blacked out, line dangling.
That's you. I gave you glasses.

THE DEATH OF IRISH

The tide gone out for good,
Thirty-one words for seaweed
Whiten on the foreshore.

MINDING RUTH

for Seamus Deane

She wreaks such havoc in my library,
It will take ages to set it right –
A Visigoth in a pinafore

Who, weakening, plonks herself
On the works of Friedrich Nietzsche,
And pines for her mother.

She's been at it all morning,
Duck-arsed in my History section
Like a refugee among rubble,

Or, fled to the toilet, calling
In a panic that the seat is cold.
But now she relents under biscuits

To extemporise grace notes,
And sketch with a blue crayon
Arrow after arrow leading nowhere.

My small surprise of language,
I cherish you like an injury
And would swear by you at this moment

For your brisk chatter brings me
Chapter and verse, you restore
The city itself, novel and humming,

Which I enter as a civilian
Who plants his landscape with placenames.
They stand an instant, and fade.

Her hands sip at my cuff. She cranes,
Perturbedly, with a book held open
At plates from Warsaw in the last war.

Why is the man with the long beard
Eating his booboos? And I stare
At the old rabbi squatting in turds

Among happy soldiers who die laughing,
The young one clapping: you can see
A wedding band flash on his finger.

HISTORY NOTES

Tonight you sat up late, fatigued, note-
Taking for tomorrow's history class,
Glossing the plague, heretical raging.
I lay back on the bed to watch your back
Stoop at the book shelf. You had asked me to
Make up a verse to occupy myself:
How close you came that moment, without knowing,
To what I do each day for the first time!
This is a starting out, insistence that –
Word by resistant word, striking for poise –
Our silences may not be spoken of.

Now you correct old copybooks, describe
Those madcap corporals cantering pell-mell
From smoke rising over small villages;
The rag-doll dead piled high in tumbrels,
Or silhouettes of chained men twitching.
But that was elsewhere and impossible:
An hour ago, I took sleep from your eyes;
My fingers on your thigh left five white marks.
Our spokesman is a festival of stillness,
Actual roses in a glass bowl pouring
Commentaries on saying nothing.

Thumbing the index of an atlas, ask me
Where Santiago de Compostela lies,
Blond shrine of a saint. Imagine pilgrims,
Frost-bitten, saddle-stiff, fasting there.

A statue's eyes wept opals every midnight,
And God bent double in a scone. But choose
The charity of rooms that are small, shut out
A clockface flinching on the mantelpiece,
Or ask a second time. I tell you, love,
We found the place long since and never left,
Staying absolutely still, still travelling.

SEÁN DUNNE

b. 1956

AGAINST THE STORM

War gathers again and the stern
Generals argue over outspread maps.
Bullets shatter the high
Pulpit where a prelate pleads.
Ministers rant on platform until
Words discard meaning and collapse.
Everywhere unease spreads like rumour.

Before it was the same, and small
Signals went unnoticed in the dark.
The gross cloud changed nothing despite
The thronged chambers, the skin
Shed like a stocking in the bomb's wake.
Afterwards, the cafés opened and stark
Lessons were unlearned. Unreal and loud,
Laughter drowned the warnings calling

Urgent as the cry of a trapped hare.
In spite of headlines now I catch
The stir of my sleeping son
Turning to begin his second year.
Against all horror I set such acts,
Intimate and warm as gathered friends
Huddled in a room against the storm
Or around the table for a final meal.

THE FIFTH BEATLE

Often I dream of you alive, an old joke
In a Hamburg basement where Beatles
Oldies spin nostalgia. The air
Is heavy as cotton with joint-smoke.
Dodging mirrors, you douse
Your face in the washroom and swear.
Your name avoids our graffiti.

Always someone has to lose, and you
Lost more than most. In Munich still,
Crowds argue on coaches from Dachau,
Claim the camp's a slur and deny
The full accounts, the ovens and labs,
Newsreels of corpses stacked on slabs.
Against that what chance have you

Who made no more than music? You live
Only in footnotes and shaky footage,
A curious appendage to the other four,
Forever on the fringe of a dead future
Where credits never carry your name
And fans refuse your memory. True
To form, they'll say we invented you.

QUAKERS

Silence takes over the room.
As if gathered for a sign, they dispatch
Business and let the moments pass.
On tables, in bowls, flowers bud
Like phrases about to be said.

57

Outside, their acre of graves
Shows names and dates like the flat
Covers of shut files. Terraces close
Around them, dogs restless in yards,
Children at windows catapulting birds.

MARMALADE AND MRS MANDLESTAM

Thank you, my dear. Marmalade, it is my childhood.
Nadezhda Mandlestam to Bruce Chatwin

To please Nadezhda in her old age
It was useless to spout in liberal rage.
Marmalade, thrillers, the best champagne,
Drew more response than relived campaigns.

Marmalade especially won her over:
A taste of life as teeming pleasure.
Its smell was girlhood, secure as shavings
Curled in a schoolbag on winter evenings.

When policemen ripped her rooms apart
For poems and books, they ignored the jar
That bound her to the world as much
As words transformed by poetry's touch

And drove her on when all seemed waste
But for the memory of that redemptive taste.

THROWING THE BEADS

A mother at Shannon, waving to her young
Son setting out from north Kerry, flung

Rosary beads out to the tarmac
Suddenly, as a lifebelt hurled from a pier.
Don't forget to say your prayers in Manhattan.
Dangling between ticket and visa,
She saw the bright crucifix among skyscrapers,
Shielding him from harm in streets out of serials,
Comforting as a fat Irish cop in a gangster film
Rattling his baton along a railing after dark.

WITTGENSTEIN IN IRELAND

He could only think clearly in the dark
So he came to Ireland, scouring Dublin
And Wicklow for shelter where thought
Would sprout in the night, a frail mushroom.

Near Arklow he wrote in a sunlit ledger.
A girl eavesdropped on pages and found
Only long words, the *schauung* and *ich*
Of whatever it was he was up to.

In Connemara he found the last pool
Of darkness in Europe, a clarity in stone
Reached like the root of a stubborn word.
Clear as theorems, sentences formed.

On my first dictionary, I wrote his truth:
*The limits of my language are the limits
Of my world*, and think of it now,
His silence a homeland I make my own.

from LETTER FROM IRELAND

for Vincent Buckley

Black sacks flapping on street corners, stiff
  Drummers walk to the Republican plot.
Behind them women in black parade with
  Flags dipped slightly. At the sacred spot
  A sheltered man proclaims a speech – *We will not
Stop struggling until the British leave.
There will be no ceasefire. We give no relief.*

Black sacks on hedges, black sacks on doors,
  Black plastic rustling as black hearses pass.
Fertiliser bags tied to electricity poles
  Signal an anger at the ultimate impasse.
  Refuse sacks, strung and stuffed, have heads to match
Thatcher or Paisley, and across a bridge some hand
Has painted in white: *Remember Bobby Sands.*

Black sacks in the doorway, black sacks in the field,
  Black rifles uncovered on a Donegal strand.
Black border on photographs, black dresses for grief,
  Black berets on coffins, black bowlers and bands,
  Black bullet holes in hallways, black words of command.
Black taxis, black jackets, black bruise and contusion.
Black crepe on a letter box, the Royal Black Institution.

Death stalks the farms of south Tyrone,
  Ruffles its cold clothes and changes
Direction for Armagh, stopping to take home
  A soldier ambushed at greeting's range.
  Nobody seems to think it strange
When Death makes some mistake and takes
As well a girl near a farmyard gate.

No matter how I try, that theme
  Slips in like fog through broken windows,
Settling on everything even if it seems
  Impossibly out of reach. Again, I forego
  My instinct for caution and let go
With rhetoric. Yet who, I ask you, could block
Misery out with the blackbird over Belfast Lough?

Echoes, echoes. That old monk in his cell
  Making from bird's cry a gloss
Is sometimes what I'd like to be, well
  Hidden by woodland, free from dross
  With nothing on my mind but women and the cross,
Watercress, berries, and a fly who'd tell
What page I stopped at in the Book of Kells.

But life is wasted searching for the pure
  Meaning of mountains or the ultimate food,
And nothing annoys me more than the dour
  Misfortunates looking for the perfect good
  In sandals and sea salt, windmills and woods
Where they stalk and tramp for purity yet
Still pause to roll a handmade cigarette.

I love instead more ordinary things
  And prefer to gaze on two women talking
Than on plants that grow as they sense you sing,
  While blokes communing with misty mornings
  Are ditchwater-dull compared to the shrill
Whistle of a train. Stuff joss sticks and ouija:
Van Morrison's worth ten of the Maharishi.

Most of what I love's more harmless and mild:
  Books, chips mixed with curry, fine
Typefaces, hurling, woodcuts, light
  Operas and spices, poker at midnight,

The inside story of gangland fights.
Not to mention Macaulay's prose and slow
Descriptions of silence by H.D. Thoreau.

In other moods I enjoy pillow-talk, say,
    Lightened by love, or the smell of old
Shops where scales tremble with weights.
    I love deserted docklands and cold
    Suburban streets where anything goes.
Mozart, I suppose, Bob Dylan if in the mood,
Ella Fitzgerald singing 'Solitude'.

My Ireland has no tin whistle wailing
    Against creels and mists on open bogs,
And neither has it place for imitation
    Thatch on houses, or for mock
    Blather to camouflage how dog eats dog.
I have no time for the view that Ireland's
The sum of the scenes at a Munster Final.

My Ireland has no dark clichéd hag
    Toothless in turfsmoke as she cackles.
I have seen the face of a woman dragged
    Through bedrooms screaming, battered
    And bruised until her body blackened.
Deirdre of the Sorrows thrives
Mostly in the home for battered wives.

The theme is changing, my rage revives.
    Memory Ireland. They shoot heroin these
Times in streets where Connolly said lives
    Were lost in slumland hunger and disease
    While gentrified suburbs sat in cushioned ease.
Archaeologists point to our early tribes
Where flatlands shelter fifty thousand lives.

So you see, dear Vincent, the outlook's bad
    Though still there's much that compensates.
The country's split in a thousand parts
    But old ideas still predominate.
    The peasant leaning on his broken gate
Is now a manager screaming for more
Grants as his workers face the lengthy dole.

Sometimes I go to Cobh and stare
    For ages at water where emigrants waved
To families on the crowded pier.
    In Manhattan or Boston, they saved
    Enough to bring another until all were there.
Old drawings depicted a country dying:
Grim men standing, shawled women crying.

The liners they left on are pictured on walls
    Of bars and hotel lounges, generations marred
By misery and the need to pour all
    Into tickets for White Star or Cunard.
    The country wears their going like a scar.
Today their relatives save to support and
Send others in planes for the new diaspora.

On the coast in west Cork once I saw
    An Indian woman throwing petals to the waves.
Water dripped from her sari, drenching her small
    Feet as she wept into water that made a grave
    For her son killed instantly in a bombed plane.
Her prayers poured over the waters gathering
And receding again. She stood in shallow lather.

Often I think of her on that rough shore
    And leave her with you now as I end,
Her hands filled with flowers and more

Meaning in the gesture than I can comprehend.
Something of what she signifies I send
To you in Australia: here dignity a sign
Sent out in defiance of her place and time.

MAIRÉAD BYRNE

b. 1957

AN INTERVIEW WITH ROMULUS AND REMUS

What did you think of the wolves?
Did they excite you?
Make you feel different? More human?
What is it like to be twins?
Did the wolves smell?
Did you find that in any way off-putting?
Did you have trouble expressing affection?
What's wolf's milk like for starters?
What were their names?
Where did they go on their holidays?
Did you find it hard to settle down again in Rome?
We call it Rome now.
I don't mean to cause a fight
but did it ever strike you that *Reme*
might have been an equally good name?
How do you boys get along?
Was it dark out there? And cold?
Are you glad to be home and how
do you get along with women, real women?
I mean, do they compare to the wolves?
Do you think your background will cause problems later in
    life?
I mean sexually.
Did you ever have it off with a wolf?
You're too young, I guess.
I don't mean to be disrespectful
but, you see, we never heard the full story.
A lot of people wonder about you boys,
being brought up by wolves and all that.
Do you miss them?
Do you know that they're nearly extinct?

Would you let your daughter marry a wolf?
How fast can you run?
Say, what's your favourite food?
Do you eat raw meat and tear it apart with your teeth?
Well, I suppose that was quite common in Rome.
Hey, thanks for your time, boys.
It's been real.
You gotta learn to talk soon, boys.
A lotta people are dying to hear about this.

GLORY DAYS

Back then I left home
to see my tom
who was holed up nearby.
We coupled in laneways –
he was that sort of guy
and I let him manhandle me.
But for all that
he was a good cat –
not quite kind, but perceptive.
Everything happened at night.
I remember the blood,
the drink, the stink of it,
the half-lived-in rooms
and both of us crying.
That was some expressionist dream
and in order to dream it
I had to be drunk –
so drunk I vomited milk
in doorways next day
as the feet of the hurrying class
beat time in Westmoreland Street.
I rode the crest of that slump

for a while, knocking around
with troublesome men.
I was going against the crowd
and sometimes people would stop me,
friends I suppose,
who said things like,
'How can you expose yourself in that way?'
'I don't know,' I would say.
I backed down
and for a few years
lost all certainty.
It was embarrassing.
Lucky my husband was there
to hide me.
I cleaned up my act.
Now I feel I'm married to everyone.
I'm everyone's mother.
We do our best to be kind
to each other and fail.
We can't even begin to explain
why it is we're fighting again.
I've grown up in fact.

THE CHRISTMAS

What we did for the Christmas
was what we do every year
though this year we tried to do more.
We got more money out of the bank –
We had more money in it so that was all right.
We got presents for everyone –
wine, sweets, lottery tickets for the kids,
nothing lavish, but nice,
and a few bob more than we usually have.
It was nothing like when we were kids.

We didn't have new clothes though we dressed up nice.
We didn't lie awake all night hoping for morning.
We didn't go on forced marches to Dollymount Strand.
We could do what we liked – we didn't even go to Mass.
There was no one we wanted to show off to –
we don't even have neighbours any more.
We didn't overeat though we ate well.
We didn't go mad for the drink though it was there for the
    taking.
We didn't fight about TV – we didn't even watch TV.
We didn't feel especially new or fresh though we felt OK.
We hadn't been cleaning the house until midnight
so we weren't exhausted.
We hadn't washed floors and put papers down
and had baths and worn American dressing gowns
and dried our hair in front of the fire.
There wasn't the same feeling of achievement,
of having arrived at something that was longed for.
It was Christmas, we were very glad of it, but that's all.
Even my mother, who's as Christmassy as mince pie,
had shipped out to the Middle East.
Good God – we didn't even have mince pies!
Our kid had everything a kid should have –
a teddy, a dress, slippers that didn't fit, some toys.
And she didn't even know it was Christmas.
How things change!
We went to the in-laws for the day
and I ate someone else's Christmas dinner.
It wasn't easy.
No one bothered to get drunk.
We're all getting old.
We never fight – not because there's nothing to fight about
but because there's a lot to be thankful for.
I nearly caused an awful fight over the Christmas
when I said I didn't think people should go to jail
for not paying their TV licence or their DART fare.

Everyone disagreed most vehemently
and there were a few tricky moments
before we became one big happy family again.

POST-NATAL WARD

It sure was intimate.
I meet women I knew then
and we don't even say hello –
I knew when their bowels moved,
when their breasts leaked,
what and how much they liked to eat,
what sorts of husbands they had
and how often,
the stuff they were made of,
how much money they had in the bank,
but never their names.
I knew their babies;
they were gazed at, compared.
I swear that I thought
each one as amazing as mine.
I inspected the ranks –
the monkey-faced one incubated,
the twins, the red-headed guy with the scabs,
the feminine boys and my masculine girl –
my spanking-new fat-legged girl!
My next-door-bed neighbour was deaf.
Her husband and children would visit,
stream in and spread out on her bed
a fiesta of rough-diamond talk.
I knew the snobs,
the ones who cut off,
the women who'd been there before
and the ones who fell down adoringly before Christ
in thanks for their child,

the women who were lying in pain,
the ones who were clipped,
the big women who loved,
who were wheeled in at night,
stunned and rekindled each time
they remembered their child.
There was no shortage of pain,
of loss, of silence, of death.
We were the elected,
the chosen few.
We were the *crème de la crème*.
My breasts spouted milk.
My whole body swaggered,
casual about its great coup.
It was so bloody glamorous!
My baby slept like a nun,
in no rush to let the world in.
I outstared the nights,
watched Dublin turn yellow and navy and pink,
and surging through me were giant peals of joy, joy, joy –
and I couldn't wait to get out.

SAINT VALENTINE'S DAY, KILKENNY

There you are, Dame Poverty,
ushering the stunted women
and their runts down past
the Castle in the cold.
You've set up shop here too,
selling bread and margarine
in slightly less than halves.
You make me feel at home –
I could live here if I got a job!
Two blond girls in summer dresses
should cheer me up.

70

Only trouble is – it's February!
They bounce their baby brother
down the street and nibble
on the cheapest chocolate cup
that three can share.
Nice town, Kilkenny.
It's so medieval.
I still can see their skinny arms,
bare as the necks of battery chicks,
thrust through the bars.
I hear them cluck beneath the barracks.
Their wives and daughters sidle up and call –
Tell him I want him!
Give him this!
The jails and churches have gone respectable.
They were built to last, of course,
and the change of ownership
has done wonders to improve opinion.
They're almost classy now.
It would take more than the bones
of prostitutes and rebels
to prise off stone from stone.
A castle can hold its breath for centuries –
and there are always little people to flourish by.

THE NEW CURRICULUM

There are things I could teach you but they can only be
    learnt over time –
how to judge when a bus might come,
how to assess the distance between stops,
when to stop looking behind and when to press on ahead,
when to cross over the road,
at what fraction of a second and at what pace,

how to relax in the middle of cars,
how to jaywalk and make it look – and feel – natural,
how to have the right change,
how not to antagonise the bus driver,
how to get him to let you off at the lights,
how to understand timing, the rhythms of city life.
How to recognise the signs of danger,
how to walk the streets at night,
how to listen for footsteps,
how to pick up your cue,
how to read faces and avert your eyes,
how to examine your neighbour at ease in bus windows,
how not to scare people,
how to queue,
how to think in the ways you have to think,
how to plan, organise,
how to act like a pro and not get left standing
when everyone else has gone home –
or somewhere better.
The city is a big place!
How to appropriate public buildings,
how to enjoy banks,
how to populate parks,
how to take short cuts through Trinity College,
how to shelter in doorways,
how to feel at home and in charge,
how not at any cost to wind up on the quays
battling with a CIE bus inspector in the rain,
ramming like an old billy and losing like hell.
Some people never learn.
There's a beauty to walking the streets,
to being a master of weaving,
a creative pedestrian.
There's a pride to handling the apparatus of a city –
the phones, the buses, the DART, the drinklink machines,
the people, oh the people!

And there's a genius to controlling breakdown,
to travelling on the upside,
to not going under.
You have to learn so many small things, subtly, over the
    years –
how to read bus numbers when your eyes fail –
I'm talking twenty-two not sixty – in these fluorescent
    days!
How to get what you want,
how to compete and remain anonymous,
how to enjoy the free things and how to deal with beggars,
how to stand on the bridge and not jump,
how to look, if not cool, at least above board,
how to attract attention in pubs,
how to know your own kind,
how many drinks you can have and get safely home,
how to sit down, approach, keep your distance, go away,
how to disentangle yourself from a chat,
how to start one and then sail away –
these, among other things, are what I have learnt.

ELEGY WITHOUT TOOTH OR HEART

Your mother shaved your head
when you had lice and sent
you back to school, a small
bald thing with worried eyes –
even your friends were ashamed.
Both of your mothers were brutes.
That's the God's honest truth –
one pushed you out, one took you in;
they did what had to be done.
There were men in there somewhere, it's true.
There were at least two,
not counting the one who smashed you up,

73

and that was an accident too.
I remember you best in your coffin.
Your sins were forgiven –
that much was clear
from the care the nuns took
in dolling you up.
You looked like a cross
between Old Mother Hubbard,
Christ's Bride,
and the Massacre of the Innocents.
All decked out in lace and blue fingernails,
with handsewn decorations on your head,
you were dead, Rosemarie.
There was a crowd of us there.
I knelt on the suave terrazzo floor
that was streaked with December slush.
I swayed on my great potato knees
and prayed to the Paraclete
for tongues of flame and miracles.
Of course nothing happened.
I smelt every ointment anyone used
and who drank and what old woman sucked drops.
My father, behind me, broke out his life's stock of tears.
Everyone's clothes were wet,
perhaps even yours,
where they hadn't quite closed you up.
The stink rose and it didn't include
the last of your little girl smells.
You still embarrassed us all.
Plucked, patched, dead as a dodo –
even the glamour of being an orphan
had gone to the bad
because the ending was grim.
I idolised and survived you.
And hey you, I have a daughter.
I named her for you, and water.

MICHAEL O'LOUGHLIN

b. 1958

THE CITY

after Cavafy

You say you will leave this place
And take yourself off to God-knows-where,
A Galway cottage, a village in Greece –
Anywhere but here:
Paris, Alexandria, Finglas,
The grey eroding suburb
Where you squandered the coin of your youth.
You wander down to the carriageway
And watch the lorries speeding by.
Swooning in their slipstreams,
You raise your eyes in a tropical dream
To the aeroplanes overhead.

But too late you realise
That you shall never leave here!
This, or next, or any other year.
You shall pass your life, grow old
In the same suburban lounge bars,
Draining the dregs of local beers,
Fingering a coin in your otherwise empty pockets.
And no matter how you toss it,
It always turns up the same:
The plastic sun of Finglas
Squatting on every horizon.
The squandered coin of your youth!
The slot machines you fed have rung up blanks,
Not just here, but everywhere.

SOME OLD BLACK SOUL WOMAN

I had the paper, I had the pen,
And I was going to tell you all about it,
To explain it all, once and for all
To lay bare my tortuous theology.
I had the words all off by heart,
My vandalised and educated
Skinny white street-punk heart:
I'm Only Trying To Be Straight With You
– We're Two Different People
Doing Our Own Thing
– We've Got Our Own Lives To Lead
This Is Nineteen Eighty-One
And then I heard the cassette
I'd put on an hour before –
Some old black soul woman,
The blues, maybe Aretha . . .
How fucking inconvenient can you get!
Some old black soul woman
Some old black soul woman
And she ain't never goin' to let me go . . .

HAMLET IN DUBLIN

The trains have stopped running
The theatres are closed
My shoulders are bruised
From the narrow corridors
That lead out onto the stage

I rehearse all night in the bars
I stagger and fall, declaiming
And O my friends

There is something rotten
In this state of ours

The car park echoes with my voice
The streetlamps blaze like footlights
And out in the darkness beyond them
I suddenly realise
There's no audience

from IN THE SUBURBS

1 A Letter to Marina Tsvetayeva

In white rooms looking out on the city
I woke up alone with you, Marina Tsvetayeva.
Her body is a sheet of cold white flame
Where I am burned to translucence;
In her hair I smelt Prague and damnation
And music tearing through flesh
Like the pull of a planet.
Her mocking schoolgirl's laugh,
Her arched dancer's calf,
Her feet in white boots like elegant hooves!

Who else
Could I pray to
To watch over her
In the darkness where she moves?

THE SMILE

Late summer. A Dublin Sunday,
hushed and heavy
my soles scrape the pavement

77

There was a smell
of burning rubber
from the park behind the flats

A policeman on a motorbike
zigzagged
the afternoon streets

a remote-control toy
smudging the air
with demon voices

A young man with a Mexican moustache
stood casual guard
as two children played in the gutter

I approached from a long way off
to ask him the way;
he answered slowly

as I watched the phoenix
sketched
on the chest of his T-shirt

'Never heard of it. But
I'll tell you this much.
It's nowhere near this kip.'

And we smiled
like the future regarding the past
or vice versa.

INTENSITY, EXALTATION

after Vallejo

I want to write, but I foam at the mouth.
There's so much to say but I get bogged down;
There's no number uttered which isn't a sum,
No pyramid written without a green heart.

I want to write, but I sense the puma;
I ask for laurel, but they give me an onion.
There's no sound made which doesn't grow vague,
There's neither god nor son of god without development.

So come on then, let's eat grass,
Fruit of weeping, flesh of moans,
Jam made out of our melancholy souls.

Come on! Come on! I am wounded;
Let's drink what's already been turned into piss,
Come on, Mister Crow, let's go to your missus.

ANNE FRANK

What we cannot speak about,
we must pass over in silence . . .

Life is lived in rooms like this.
That, at least, we can say.
And people come and go
On speakable missions,
Clear commands. And we can talk
And smother the air with words
Till we feel we understand.

In these rooms we sleep and dream,
And rise to breakfast on white linen.
There are books to read,
And at night the scratch
Of pen and paper.

Life is lived in rooms like this
Where we lean towards a square of light
But where the walls are
We can only discover
By walking out into that darkness,
Fingers outstretched, blind,
Knowing we have no words
For what we may find.

ON HEARING MICHAEL HARTNETT READ HIS POETRY
  IN IRISH

First, the irretrievable arrow of the military road
Drawing a line across all that has gone before,
Its language a handful of brutal monosyllables.

By the side of the road the buildings eased up;
The sturdy syntax of castle and barracks,
The rococo flourish of a stately home,

The formal perfection and grace
Of the temples of neoclassical government,
The avenues describing an elegant period. Then,

The redbrick constructions of a common coin
To be minted in local stone, and beyond them
The fluent sprawl of the demotic suburbs

Tanged with the ice of its bitter nights
Where I dreamt in the shambles of imperial iambs,
Like rows of shattered Georgian houses.

I hear our history on my tongue,
The music of what has happened!
The shanties that huddled around the manor,

The kips that cursed under Christ Church Cathedral
Rising like a madrigal into the Dublin sky
– But tonight, for the first time,

I heard the sound
Of the snow falling through moonlight
Onto the empty fields.

BRENDAN CLEARY

b. 1958

BORN AGAIN

get thee behind me Creeping Jesus,
Mary, Joe the Carpenter & all the saints

fetch me vodka – large measures!
& skin up that spliff old buddy
Lucifer – shall we check out a club?

may all my hangovers be guiltless
my love affairs dim & witless

scrumpy, homegrown coke,
mad orgies thru the night

gimme gimme gimme
gimme gimme gimme

I'VE SEEN THE LIGHT . . .

SCRATCHMARKS

I've heard toothpaste
removes love bites –
at least a salesman
I hitched from Knutsford
Services told me so,
and he drove a Volvo
with buttons to adjust

reclining seats
and headrests,
so who was I to doubt?

What I wanted to know, though,
was what would happen
if his suspicious wife –
from what he told me
her passion was more for
double-layer cream cakes
than Charlie's flights of fancy –
what would happen if
returning albeit reluctantly
from some foreign trip,
having secured orders
to secure in turn
new garage doors,
new patio furniture
and Jason's ski trip,
if he, the wild rover,
had dirty great big
scratchmarks from some
thin Belgian hussy
on his spider-like back
or inside arm?

'Easy,' he said,
cruisin' past juggernauts
like Steve McQueen.
'Easy . . .
I'd just say it was quiet
and all the men were desperate,
so competing for contracts
we wrestled a bit together . . .'

HOME BREW & VIDEO

turns out
we could have made it
to the Speedway after all,
but we just couldn't raise ourselves
once we'd settled down.
Completely lethal stuff!

i was scanning the papers
with malice,
next thing i know
she'd sprawled across me,
cuddled up!

i sneered
at right-wing bias
& she tittered,
rising as usual
to fiddle a bit
with the knobs . . .

GROUNDS OF ASYLUM

I've seen them often as I cross the lawn,
their dishevelled committee meeting
beneath drooping branches.
They sit on benches bestowed to them
by last century's gentlemen.
Strange, I should always notice
their white stubble, how short
they wear their cast-off trousers.
Murmuring, they always seem to stare
like nomads to an aimless distance.

Indeed from over here, in the new block,
they could be mistaken for scarecrows
flapping their arms at pigeons.
I laugh when I see them on trains
or buses, disrupting clerks or shoppers,
ranting about Vikings.
Their grinning faces always make me
want my childhood back . . .

MORE THAN COFFEE

in the future
you will be owned
by a cruel government

you may have to
dig the soil
there will be no intimacy
it will be forgotten

it's a poor excuse, i know,
but i'm a man of morals

so may i
may i please
stay the night . . .

DEVILS

And so we meet again
after tiffs & scuffles
in your pine kitchenette.

Why is it, i wonder,
i feel only this urge,
this ridiculous urge
to rearrange the atmosphere?
Think i'll smash up
all your poxy jam jars
crammed with rice & lentils,
with those woeful ADUKI beans.

Later, like the speaking clock,
you'll still be prattling
down here oblivious in the débris,
while i'll be upstairs
muttering PROPERTY IS THEFT
in your lavish bathroom
or maybe upturning beds
hunting out Daddy's
priceless antique knickknacks,
hurling them with glee
like paper planes,
aiming them straight
at your sensitive cats
with their pretentious names
as they skulk in the yard
near the patio door . . .

COMRADES

Can't get through to the comrades
on the telephone.

They must be listening in again
at the state exchange.
Bureaucrats!

Their network of cables
and wires that stalk us.

It's a shame
I can't get through to the comrades.
We have much to discuss,
the flattening of office blocks,
the liberation of factories.

DERMOT BOLGER

b. 1959

from FINGLAS LILIES

III February 1981

steel winds at dawn sting like a wasp
in this factory where men are cursing
and rust grows like hair on a corpse

she's off to work as I finish night-shift
today is our child's first birthday
I'll put his name on the housing list

taking a chair I sit in the garden
smoking Moroccan dope and tripping
the housing estate is disappearing

I feel I'm at the bottom of a pond
floating below rows of water lilies
with new names like Finglas & Ballymun

from FINGLAS BALLADS

III Auld Lang Syne

this Christmas is six days old
all our baby's toys are broken
there's a gang out on the road
trying to force car doors open

but come on girl it's New Year's Eve
at Christ Church we can hear the bells
in those crowds you can make believe
next year we'll have escaped this hell

these are the streets I used run
steeplechasing 'cross people's lawns
learning to fight when night had come
learning to love down lanes at dawn

now kids look at me coming from work
they whisper like I was a stranger
we're lodgers in your mother's house
building borders through our anger

but come on girl it's New Year's Eve
we can dance in the street at twelve
one slap of metal and we'll believe
the cries of birth from the bells

STARDUST

Last night in swirling colour we danced again
and as strobelights stunned in black and white
I reached in this agony of slow motion for you
but you danced on as if cold light still shone
merging into the crowd as my path was blocked
by snarling bouncers & the dead-eyed club owner

When I screamed across the music nobody heard
I flailed under spotlights like a disco dancer
and they formed a circle clapping to the beat
as I shuddered round the club in a violent fit
hurling through a dream without trembling awake
I revolved through space until I hit the ground

Lying among their feet tramping out the tunes
I grasped you inside my mind for this moment
your white dress bobbing in a cool candleflame
illuminating the darkness spinning towards me

a teenage dancing queen proud of her footwork
sparks rising like stardust all over the floor

from THE MAN WHO STEPPED OUT OF FEELING

5 The Watcher's Agony

The devil is in this room tonight. He wants us.
Cups rattle in your mind and the table levitates.

I hold onto your body as if trying to protect you
but the terror trapped in your imagination escapes.

Can you hear a word I say or even feel my presence?
I cannot grasp what is disintegrating under my arms

where you shudder wedging yourself into my shoulder
and then speak in a voice estranged from your own.

The devil is in this room tonight. Inside both of us:
everything we ever suppressed attacks the furniture.

When I black out into sleep I dream I am still awake
and you lean above me choking on words I cannot hear.

This room has broken loose from the harbour of reality
through your unchecked flood of tears it is buffeting.

The devil you see frantically tugging the smashed helm
as he turns with wild hair in the spray is his face mine?

MARCH 1983

I AM IRELAND

after Pearse

'Nursing – Young Ladies over 17½ years required for Gt
Britain. *Free Fares.* Facilities for religious duties.' – 1948

'750,000 men and women have left Ireland since 1922.' –
April 1959

I am Ireland
Older I am than Birmingham's tower blocks
    From a land disowning me
    To this city not my own
    The first ache of exile

Great was my pride
When they taught me of Cuchulainn at school
    Twelve hours scrubbing the wards
    Then the jammed ballroom floor
    Irish phrases echo in limbo

Great was my shame
My own people disinherited their daughter
    Jolted from cover by the bombing
    Into the final exile of whispers
    In my son's acquired accent

I am Ireland
Lonelier I am than a hag on Birmingham Common

SNUFF MOVIES

The wind shuffles through the cracked glass and the
    floorboards rot.
It has been eight days since I stepped outside this filthy flat
where I've sat watching and four times my vigil has been
    rewarded:

four times I have hung within the limbo of the static from
the tube,
longing for release and yet not daring to believe it could
happen,
and four times the picture hasn't jerked back on to
advertisements –
my throat has dried up and my body trembled as I
watched
the figure thrown naked into the room and the beating
begin.
Whole days wither stagnantly in this flat and nothing
happens,
days when I'm stuck like an insect on fly paper unable to
move,
trapped within the metallic hiss of that ocean of static,
and I wait and pray that the advertisements will not
continue
as over and over the slogans repeat without commentary or
pity,
hammering out messages at those remaining sealed in their
rooms.
Once we walked down streets and worked in throbbing
factories,
I remember oil on my overalls and the smell of sweat
without fear,
but then the coalitions collapsed and regrouped and were
submerged
by the corporations who had learnt how to survive without
us.
Just four times the knife has flashed like an old matador's
and youngsters raised their heads although blinded by the
hood.
There is no way of knowing how many of my workmates
are left,
caged up before crackling boxes terrified to miss the
murders.

Last month I saw a man run with a plastic bag through the
  litter,
apart from him all streets to the superstore were deserted.
I breathe safely – I am too old for anybody's attention,
they will never come and shove me hooded into that
  studio,
I will never strain my head forward in expectation of the
  blow.
From this final refuge I can spy and be involved in their
  agony,
the flesh wincing and that final anonymous moan of pain;
and afterwards I breathe again in my renewed triumph of
  living.
Nobody knows any longer when the curfew begins or ends
but one evening I heard them come for somebody on the
  street.
I never knew which hooded neighbour I might have once
  passed
kept the whole of Ireland contained for a day with their
  death.
I know they are killing me too in this war of nerves I
  survive in,
it's been years since I've not slept sitting upright in this
  chair
dreaming of blood and waking fretfully to advertisements,
and yet I still cling on, speaking to nobody in the
  superstore,
running home frantic that I will miss a final glimpse of life.
Long ago I believed in God – now I believe what I am told:
there is no heaven except that instant when the set comes
  alive,
no purgatory except the infinite static bombarding the
  screen,
hell could only be if they came for the television or for me.

HALIFAX, NOVA SCOTIA

for Anthony Cronin

Smooth as death
  The packed ice shone
    Across an alabaster oblivion

When he looked up
  He could not fathom
    What landscape he travelled on

He closed his eyes
  But could only remember
    Passports and baggage handlers

And some motor advertisement
  Glimpsed on an escalator ride –
    Life may be short but it is wide.

The murmuring voices
  In the airport coach
    Might have spoken any language

And all he could discern
  Through the frozen window
    Was the shape of five letters

Scorching the blackness
  (Like encroaching crosses
    Of the Ku Klux Klan

Or a frontier post for Hell)
  Framing the solitary red word
    H O T E L

PETER SIRR

b. 1960

YORICK

Regard the empty, quizzical sockets,
The hushed cavities into which
My substantial laughter has reverted
But do not patronise me with dwarfish
Rhetoric. Here the courts are helpless
My leisurely gibes so undo
Doublets and hose, debatable crowns.

Ashen kings stalk endless battlements
And nervous heirs go babbling of murder,
Failing to notice the stars dispatch
A condescending light,
Failing to read in comic skulls
How predictably the states rot.
For this bloody, repetitive hell

Doubles, Hamlet, as the paradise of fools
Who have no need now of deformities
And are grown so magnificent
We humble the proven genealogies.
Here the royal lines meet. Committing,
Recommitting privileged crimes, they rail
Against the heaven of the incorruptible.

Laertes proceeds with such a tragic air.
Your hands are trembling, prince. A bitter wind
Disperses your hair. Why did you come back?
Deadly neuroses blow through Elsinore,
No one is immune. Forget
Godliness, the fury of the disinherited,
It does not matter any more.

GUIDO CAVALCANTI TO HIS FATHER

How will I know you where you lie
Low among the dog-tagged
Prisoners of iron and fire
Or how, hearing only
The agreed text into which
Their solitary cries cohere,
Will I distinguish
Your tiny paradigm of pain?

Nonetheless I draw near, borne
Through special categories of despair
Towards my own sins' region.
I bear to the unappeased
Bulletins from the upper air,
Impossible memories stowed
In a little fleet of images.
What do I hope to salvage here?

Yet I would stagger again up the beaches
Of those flawed havens
Where we who hardly dared collide
Delicately improvised,
Building trust like huts from driftwood;
I would endure again each silent storm,
Words like provisions under sand
Or maps of lands we strained to find

And each attempt at reparation
That proved a shyer kind of failure.
If they should find each other
Let our eyes, like vying households,
At last abandon ruse and armour
Having nothing now to lose
In this later kingdom, father,
Where no one hesitates.

IN THE JAPANESE GARDEN

The little red bridges
Have nothing to tell
Of exact endearments,

Kimonos rustling in the breeze.
The fate of millions
Was never settled here

Though the rare flowers bow
And in the hierarchic waterfall
Every drop knows its place.

A Wicklow wind clicks
In bamboo that has never hurried
Through staked-out prisoners

And if we can never replace
The inscrutable shoguns
Who should be here

Babbling of honour among
The fag-ends and Coke tins
Our local samurai

Are coming on.
More and more accurately
They test their penknives

And their girls
On the educational exotica,
In the peeling pagodas.

97

'The range is French and has a mind of its own.
All night long the turf crumbles in the airtight
Chamber and the hot ash rains on the tray
Yet morning finds the needle stuck at zero
And I come stumbling through the kitchen door,
The last of the true pioneers, arms laden
With firelighters and tins of beans, watching
Through the window the smoke of a dozen
Competent valley fires lean towards Maam.

'After breakfast I follow the sunlight
Round the room and copy out my phonemes.
I sit for hours in their homes, a casual
Interloper listening for the square brackets
In the conversation, observing how
The troublesome genitive falls into disuse
In an afterglow of language. Looking up,
I see a trawler heading for the tiny pier,
The white foodmarket stark against the bay

'And wonder why I'm here, making coffins
For words. Yesterday I climbed awkwardly
To the top of the hill behind the house
Past two famine cottages and an ageing
White mare looking down into the valley
Like a receding myth, coming at last
To a pile of stones left for someone killed.
When I came down the fire had gone out . . .
On windy days I stay inside and watch

'A lone tree grow sideways like something dreamed
Or the idea of a tree, imperfectly grasped,
Which the wind has brought from a country
Where trees are possible. Each hopeful branch

Migrates eastward to where the light falls
The right way up, in orchards, textbook meadows
Or in slow encroaching shadows round hooded
Monastery gardens where night shimmies down
The perfect canopies like an unzipped skirt.

'Out on the margins the serious stars
Like drinkers gather, flashing sudden wit
Above the huge abandoned rocks,
The phone wires lying heavy on the poles.
My aerial's angled to the moon
As I prick my ears to the shaky news:
In three dialects the old people die
And the lights come on in local halls.
A volleyball team is making major strides.'

LANDSCAPES

I'm growing fat on heather and fern,
The ponderous think-bubbles
Of clouds in a western sky.

Who'd have thought the gods so woolly?
All day the sky fills with heavy-handed
Theories not one of them

Can find the right words for
While the Twelve Pins of Connemara
Doze in the distance

And Lettermore palms the bay.
I think of seals and stones,
Oblique treasures gone to ground

In placenames: Roundstone, Recess.
The Clifden bus,
A blurred red daub

In somebody's chancy pursuit of light,
Hits an air-pocket . . .
None of this

Is worth the flatter lands I could devise,
Perpetual midlands glimpsed
From the tradesman's entrance

Of a passing train, with nothing for the eye
To settle on but meadows pulling back
And the little stone stations

Whose names are longer than their platforms.
You are getting down at one of these,
You are wrapped with smiles

As with the rug around your knees.
Or you have stayed aboard to read,
As the steam thins, the dates on sleepers,

The curtains closing on a back bedroom.

SMOKE

You will be always coming back here to inhale
the tobacco skies of Groningen, spreading yourself
sleepily above the *halfzwaar* November
of Theodorus Niemeyer, hugging the masts
of the restaurant moored in the black canal.
Graffiti flutters on the block nearby

and I'll be repeating myself too,
still asking directions, having returned to haunt
my three weeks' haunting of you here, or prove
this city real, hoping to discover
the one street you never found or in which
we somehow forgot to hold hands; hoping to hear
the toytown tolling of the Martinitoren
and march out into the square unmoved.
I'll be waking on the tremor of your brushstroke,
chancing a finger on your back. And later,
the table's theatre of absence: orange halves
like Aztec hearts, a curl of ham
in an ashy spill of toast, my hand
lifting the glass dome
to gash the Gouda, my lips
already drifting from butcher to baker
on the words you lend me that raise a smile
and know me still your creature.

FLY

A bluebottle has buzzed in to settle
on my father's face. Why not here
as anywhere? It crawls on the greyed face
and hops and flits, filling the little room with its noise
which is like any other, the scratch of footsteps
on the sun-loosened tarmac
of the mortuary car park, the buried groan of traffic
through the open door. And we add ours, the darting
blankness of grief, a panicked cry
dying quickly in the city air, the Carmelites'
perfunctory stream of prayer, the fly of ritual
which touches everything and stays nowhere.

TALK, TALK

Why am I always trying
to make you say things?
As if all our life had been
this one conversation hovering
over a broken microphone . . .

I have fallen back on notes
that thin out as I read,
I had drunk too much to listen
or I have forgotten.
I have thrown

everything to the wind but caution.

VIGILS

Something of me is still there, held forever
in the white light of a difficult room, the air
all constraint, a thinness; something useless:
a hand lifted into space, getting nowhere,
a word dying in its bed of language

and often I'd turn to you with a righteous magic
turning love to air, hugging grief
like a toy. But lying here this morning
watching the light grow on your cheek
in the seconds I love, before the clock shrieks

and your skinny shoulders come to life
in my palms, I felt something stir, some gentle pressure
as if my father had pushed the air aside
with mild impatience, reaching down the light
to where we lay.

Listen to me now. Why do you never listen?

ANDREW ELLIOTT

b. 1961

ONE OF LAURA MARX'S LETTERS

He who is against hunger, he who is for mountains of bread,
should take up the hammer in the spirit of youthful joy so that
no engine remains unrepaired.

Rosta window, 1920

In this letter written after her marriage –
In the middle of her life – I hear her
Complain that a crabby landlady
Will not light a fire for her, her husband
And her sick baby. She is maligned by small things.

Curled up under the blankets that have moths in them,
Her brain becomes like a fieldmouse asleep
At the roots of the corn, then weaving the ground,
Dribbling in and out the trunks of stalks,
Finding manifestos pinned up there.

One hundred years later the harvesters
Are circling her on the vast wheat fields of Russia,
Their mechanical blades slicing and slicing
The precious hosts of corn, the tremoring heads,
Until her mind jumps awake to her baby crying.

So, with a special lens to look back between the lines
I can see her busy in that middle-of-the-night room,
How already there is a suicide note on the table
Beside the porcelain jug she dabs towels into
And then sets them on his forehead to ease the fever.

CLEANLINESS

In weeks of solitary confinement, during three and a half years
in prisons and prison camps, she scratched her poems with a
spent match on pieces of soap, then committed them to memory.

Washing her hands of the poem she has just written,
It becomes a stone sinking to the floor of her mind
Where it settles gently onto the cairn of other stones
That has grown like a faith clotting in her memory
Through the years of her life when a microphone
Has listened to her day and night like a pinprick
In the integument that separates her from a guard
In shirt sleeves, sipping tea in a cabin bristling
With electric, his head reverberating with heavy
Breathing and his eyes glazed over this day's *Truth*,
While outside his window the wind scavenges
Like a wolf whittled down by the cold to its fangs
Slavering off into the sunset – that gracious blush
Of pink dissolving through the cosmos like a disc of soap.

EAVESDROPPING

With my eyes closed I am listening
To her breathing after she has gone to sleep.
It is like slipping a piece of tissue paper
Between her head and the pillow –

Into that middle distance
Where her thoughts ripple and settle
And leave an imprint of the day.
If she opens one eye it is to say

'Can't you *ever* leave me alone?'

RODIN'S HEADACHE

*But there was one muse/mistress above all others, Camille
Claudel . . . Unlike the rest, she was herself a gifted sculptor;
and she had a mind and desires of her own . . . Rodin met her
in 1883, when she was twenty and a student. The relationship
lasted fifteen years; her face and form appear repeatedly in his
works of those years – including the nude studies at the very
top of 'The Gates of Hell'.*
Edwin Mullins

Holding his head in her hands like a phrenologist,
She is feeling through that meagre mane of hair
For all the little bumps of his genius – the skull
Beneath the skin, the softness of his temples,
The little things he never notices or bothers with –
Until now, with a flick of his wrist, he waves her off

Without thinking; back into the middle of their studio
With its marmoreal walls and its windows rattling
Under the enormity of a tumultuous Paris sky
In which the clouds are split in only one place
By a sleeve of gold and from out of which –
Like the benevolent right arm of God

Showing off the work of his child to another God –
A single shaft of light shines in upon the statues
Of 'Balzac' or 'The Thinker', gilding them like saints,
But in doing so leaves her among the shadows and
    draughts
Her mind is weaving into a shawl that she drapes
Around her shoulders and clutches at her throat

For the cold comfort it can give her as she squats
In the dawn of a new century of Art, her fingertips
And toes and the tingling tightness of each nipple
Atrophying under his eyes as they probe her
To the core, before he picks up his chisel
And puts the finishing touch to a work in marble.

PEEPSHOW

In resurrection they neither marry,
nor are they given in marriage,
but are like the angels of God in Heaven.
                                        Mark 12:25

Lying there with you, Hannah, under the antique quilt
We'd bought ourselves for a special Christmas treat,
And as my mind dissolved into *la petite mort* –
Bits drifting off like islands through the cosmos
That was pitch dark and tingling with starlight –
Before long I was standing with my pale hands cupped
To the window of an eighteenth-century cottage
In what – for some reason or another – I knew
To be a colony of the Shakers; the air and the sky
So stiff with light that it was hard at first
Seeing in through the small square panes encrusted
With salt off an ocean – a glitter of crystals
That dissolved with my breath until I could see in
To where there were women at work –
Some old, some young, some in between –
Everything motionless but for the spritely flickering
Of needles through the scraps of common cloth
On a quilt donated by a convert from France,
While behind them in a doorway stood Mother Ann,
Her eyes, Hannah, fixed on me, ecstatic and opalescent,
And when she opened her mouth there came only
The sounds of babies – gurgling, crying, squealing,
    laughing –
So out of this world, Hannah, it jumped my mind awake
Bolt upright in our bedroom in cosmopolitan
    New York . . .

And yet when I'd recovered, gone out to the loo
And come back in, relaxed and drained,
I couldn't help but wonder, Hannah,

106

If any of those women really had in the end
Ever made it to the life beyond –
As all of them must certainly have expected to.
In fact, Hannah, I wondered if they had been watching us
Just then, imagining them all perhaps grown young again
And crowded in their silk-white gowns to a tear
In the threadbare clouds of heaven,
Each jostling with her elbows, their wings in the way,
As under lamplight and two hundred years on
We cavorted over their labour of love –
Two bedroom gymnasts with our heads full of
The Function of the Orgasm and with no thoughts at all
For God or piety like them, like the little French one
Whose bony face pokes through with her skin gone
Yellowish in the gold light like wax, translucent
With sanctity and concern . . . I pull her quilt up over us
And smile as I taste again your juices on my tongue;
With the milk-weight of your breast in my palm
I am lulled by the sirens threading through Manhattan
As Mother Ann draws down the blinds on Shaker-heaven
And off it floats – a dream-bubble diminishing into space.

JOHN HUGHES

b. 1962

DOUBLE INDEMNITY

She watches him drop dead
over the pay phone

in the lobby of
the Parador Hotel.

But his uncanny foresight
has provided for her.

Tomorrow a Belfast
flying on one engine

will drop her supplies:
a bale of Durban Poison

and a ten-dollar Airedale
by the name of Fritz.

I believe she'll be content –
Miss Stanwyck or Mrs MacMurray,

or whatever her name is.

TELL-TALE

She was leaving town
in spite of herself.
Tell-tale Downpatrick

had taken its toll
over the year and day
she'd called it home.

I'd give her a dirty needle
as she put on her face
in her roof-top hidey-hole –
O she would whimper
and she would moan
and I'd become her beau,

for I know her too well
to think she'd find joy,
contentment, or whatever,
out of reach of the charms
I am almost famous for –
believe me, believe me.

A RESPECT FOR LAW AND ORDER

for Dermot Seymour

The general will be shot in the face
when his new chauffeur forgets orders
and stops for a red traffic light.
Within the hour one of the usual suspects
will be rounded up and taken downtown
to an interrogation room on the tenth floor
of the National Central Security building;
and after five hours of electric shocks
and beatings with a length of rubber hose
he will be ordered to open the window
and step outside for a breath of fresh air.

He will fall head-first onto a crowded pavement
of journalists, pickpockets, private detectives,
air-force pilots, French polishers, jazz-guitarists,
civil servants in the Department of Information,
elderly women on their way across town
to visit their latest grandchild,
young men sauntering to a soccer match
between the national side and Paraguay,
a famous Italian new expressionist painter,
and the newly arrived cultural attaché
of the Republic of South Africa.

The suspect will then pick himself up,
take a look at himself in the nearest window,
tuck in his shirt, straighten his tie,
and disappear into the leafy suburb
where he lives in a modest apartment
with his second wife and her two children;
and finish the book he was reading
when interrupted by an old school friend
dressed to the nines in a uniform
he had recently come to respect.

DADA

Someone followed the spots of blood
from his bedside to the kitchen

where he had collapsed face first
into the sizzling frying pan

of bacon, mushrooms and eggs
she had been cooking

before taking hold of herself
to become his daughter again:

never again *Daddy's little girl*
when all the lights go out

and the house is as quiet
as two voices will allow.

PURITANS AND CAVALIERS

The débris of a late-night argument:
a broken reading lamp, a smashed glass.
The contents of an ashtray cover the TV.
You appear dressed in black and white
and enquire if I am willing to discuss
what we had bawled at one another
when half-stoned and completely drunk.
But as I try and gather myself to speak
you say you're late for work and must rush,
and if I'm still interested we'll talk later.

I clean the TV with salt and water
and watch Schrader's *Hardcore* on video.
When it's all but over I return to bed
and phone you to arrange a lunchtime rendezvous
in the grounds of the City Hall,
for it's vital I understand once and for all
how unnatural some of my practices are.
What are the questions to be answered?
Are you a puritan? Am I a cavalier?
Breathless, I lie among a pile of your underclothes.

111

FLAME

When the Dance of the Firebird ended
He brought her to the Lady-chapel
To cool down in supernatural silence.
She lit a candle and prayed to the flame
That she be spared another speech
About the need to trust one another
When nothing is as it first appears
In the silences between cold sheets.

'Do they love us, those whom we love?'
It was a question she thought as tender
As anything that had passed his lips
In the year she had been the servant
Of his immature, decadent, ruinous nature.
Full of apprehension and sadness she asked him,
'Why must it always end this way?'
And he had thoughts of separateness and revenge.

CASSANDRA

As the express pulled out of the station
the young woman sitting opposite me said,
'The world will end within the hour,
when a baboon and an idiot-girl couple
in the lift of the Hôtel des Bons Enfants.
As the poet commanded, *Thou shalt not love
by ways so dangerous.* Do you not concur?
Am I making what you would call nonsense?'

She laid her head in my lap and cried
for ninety-nine kilometres.
When we arrived in the Gare du Nord
she screamed, 'Wrong again. And somehow,

Monsieur Irlandais, it is your fault.
Do you have no conscience or regret?'
Only then did I notice the tumours on her face –
the blood trickling out of every orifice.

FAIRYTALE DOCTORS

They shine a pencil light in my left eye
and tell a joke about 'I' and 'You'.

They throw salt in my face.
A grain lodges in my third eye
and I glimpse Ptolemy's *Adri deserta*
sinking under the weight of 114 dragonflies.

They breathe fire on me.

They lay eggs on my charred tongue.

BABYLON TIDE

Mrs Babylon spoke in a soft voice
about youthful happiness and uncertain love.
'Where do I begin and end?'
she asked as we reached the water's edge
and the last thirty seconds of summertime.

She went out with the tide
to be washed up further down the coast
with the Black Death, Leviathan,
a splinter of the One True Cross,
the heads of Ursa Major and Ursa Minor.

THE CHILL WIND

Because the chill wind ordered me
I opened the triple-locked door
To the malnourished Kathleen.

And then the wind insisted
I take her to a restaurant
Whose gazpacho makes insomniacs
Of everyone who clears their bowl.

Through the night of December 21st
We debated Bachelard's opinion
That cold is a symbol for solitude.

Next morning she slept through the thaw
I had negotiated with the wind,
After promising it a door in my house
To bang open and shut for ever.

PETER McDONALD

b. 1962

At last there was time to dream again,
or it seemed that way at least.
The sunset had changed only slightly
since yesterday, but it had changed.

The photograph he tried for became
a letter, and the letter became ash
in his own hearth before long,
even before the sun had set.

There was always something else to be caught,
or there would be soon, with luck.
His fire burned like the sun in Florida

where, slightly drunk by now, the last
astronaut alive was still wondering
how to make his way back to the moon.

from UNNATURAL ACTS

3 Galatea

Each night when they bring her face to face
with her torturers, when she
and the branding iron come cheek to cheek,
he's in his box, watching from behind a curtain,
and before retrieving his coat and top hat
from the headless lackey, will have closed
his eyes just as she and the hot iron

115

kiss, opening them in time for her screams
and the rest of the action, live on stage.

Is he quite sure she felt no pain?
Alone at night in his private chamber
of horrors, locked in with her waxwork double,
he gives his doctor's hands
the run of her body, smoothing out
blemishes and talking as a lover might do,
allowing himself one classical allusion
as he starts to unbutton Galatea's dress,
biting the wax, abject, *surréaliste*.

OUT OF IRELAND

Just how far do you have to go
before you get to the world's edge?
Today, a hard sun lights the snow
for miles, and deep inside his cage

your tame canary sings and dances,
ignoring winter. He has a voice
and uses it, taking no chances.
He entertains, as though he had a choice.

This summer you'll be sailing west,
whether the sea is calm or angry,
until you drop. Your bird knows the rest,
he knows he'll die hungry.

PLEASURES OF THE IMAGINATION

Again I'm caught staring
at the sky, in particular

those blue-black clouds
that shadow the sun. I remember
I was meant for a painter
and see in a puddle
cause for reflection.

I've packed my bags again
for cloud-cuckoo-land;
you might see me there,
mouth agape, as I recline
on beds of asphodel,
finally reaping the benefits
of a classical education.

But there are other approaches;
the celebrated Donal O'Sheugh
owes his allegiance
to a different culture.
He has carpeted his apartment
in the heart of New Jersey
with the best Irish turf

(perhaps, all the time,
he was speaking in parables).
Not that it matters –
I think I could stay here
amazed by this September
sun-shower, quite silent,
until his cows come home.

Meanwhile, on a deserted
filmset, the handsome
Count Dracula has heard tell
that he is a metaphor now,
and is unhappy.

He aspires to symbolism
and perhaps, one day, to nothing at all.

KILLERS

You could think of them as hunters,
achieved, professional,
ready for anything.
Their minds are on the job in hand
and their hands are steady.
They've gone by now, most likely,

but in the country, one by one,
the birds are falling
out of the trees, into
another shade of green;
just sparrows, thrushes,
nothing exceptional,

at least nothing you'd notice
in this weather, walking
the wet road home
at closing time, until
there are hands on your arm,
light as feathers.

A SHORT HISTORY OF THE WORLD

for John Hughes

It begins with another non sequitur,
a man and a woman talking,
getting nowhere fast. They're sure

of one thing only, that they're walking,
however slowly, right out of the picture,
just that one thing.
It follows, by and large, from there,
until the man in the hat walks in,
saying he's just come back from the interior.

The rest is history again, in fact
his starring role of 1948
in MGM's *Short History of the World*
(a flop), another film or two, then back
to the first obscurity. Tonight's late
movie shows him at his best though,
out in the cold and on the run,
cornered apparently in a blind alley
and trying to strike dud matches in the rain.

THE GREEN, GRASSY SLOPES OF THE BOYNE

Or, alternatively,
the Braniel Housing Estate.
The postman at the garden gate
hovers (except that for me
there is no gate, and the garden
is grass rubbed dead, and dog turds),
hovers, and tells me he's no postman
(I never catch the exact words,
maybe it's a park warden).
At any rate, he makes it known
that he has come today,
no, to deliver nothing. To send away.

But nothing changes here, or never has:
a few times snow
has covered the whole garden. When I show

119

him the photographs of myself
standing up fat and smiling
against that year's white-out,
all he can do is look away again.
I pull him back, show him
the whole extent of change
in a garden that, in any case,
was never his to cultivate,
winter or summer, one step beyond the gate.

That Friday, looking down
at a city greyed out by smoke
rising with its own sound,
thud after thud, and all the time
a choir of sirens
swooping to work, I was standing
right at the very centre of the garden
while indoors the radio
announced, interpreted, till its voice broke.
The sun set as it always does, lighting
the hills and burning up clouds like rags.
They were gathering the dead in plastic bags.

This time, again, he's leading me
up that same garden path
to a familiar height, where I can see
down years, without any photograph,
to myself and others marching, beating
hard toy drums and dragging past
The green, grassy slopes of the Boyne.
When I come back
to the corner, I turn and start again.
The clouds are burning like photographs
all over again
and I turn around and go back, and around and back
    again.

PATRICK RAMSEY

b. 1962

TABLEAU FOR THE NEW YEAR

A picture scene, so let's paint.

The turn of the year. The snow
Is no longer falling & the light
Rushes – no shadow, no remembrance,
A handful of simple perspectives.

Beneath the damp, the colourless sky,
The houses – grey-slated, rufous-bricked –
Ponderously await, the windows long
And blue in their quietness.

Yet visible, the cobblestones
& the tramlines. We are travelling
Towards the three-roaded junction.
We pass the graveyard, the empty park.

Angered, you ignore me & stare
Into the distance, a distance
Not unlike a lavender heath,
Or – better still – a purple fell

Covered in gorse or whin, a mist
Of chill after-rain, stillborn winds,
A mist close like a thought bearing
A certain resonance.

And I want to touch your shoulder,
The hem of your lilac shawl,
And watch your turning towards me.
Face crescent and profile. Face full

Against the houses and the snow,
Against the trot of the horses,
The suddenness of civic institutions.

I want to see your eyes
In modest/immodest laughter, a bird of
No open-ended song,

Thus & thus alight
With a termination of silence,
Unfalling snows.

RETREAT

Just myself, the Cavehill.
Height, the after-feeling
of driving rain, a bare dawn.
Mud and clouded breath.

The nth station. Birdsong.
The harsh caws of jays, magpies –
their cold flight a guess
in a scrub of ruined trees.

Looking below, the city
is no longer what it is –
Presbyterian, the poet's
unchanging touchstone –

but stripped, pared
with mist and distance,
the otherness of silence.
Towers, churches. A lough.

Bridges to anonymous quarters,
like the pencil strokes
of a strange, virtuous poet –
accents, stresses, caesuras,

like a living cipher
towards a new translation
of uncertain, scattered tongues,
a page of possible glosses.

FOR CERTAIN POETS

Your gift, not how to live, but how to see
The unnerving, fruitful conspiracy

Of common things: journeys, hurried letters,
Shopping, sniping at your literary betters,

Your liking for Scotch whisky, jazz and blues,
Or standing appalled at the latest news,

You depict this crass yet wonderous age
With quiet markings upon the blank page

Spoken with a tempered, a restrained voice,
Teaching man not just to sorrow, but rejoice.

Life has good things. Show them to the light!
Ideas pulled carefully like a kite,

Thrown to the heavens yet strung to earth
By the old subjects: love, death, a child's birth,

Crafted naturally with the poet's art
To find their echoes in the reader's heart.

By praising the good book, that woman's fuss,
You add to the clutter of each lived-in house . . .

THOUGHT AT CENTRAL STATION

Sunday evening. A railway terminus.
Death, you feel, must be
Something like this.

Not, you understand,
Like the end of a journey
Or even its beginning,

But rather the confluence
Of silence and trapped sunlight,
The feeling of a certain aimlessness.

AN AFTERNOON IN THE PARK

Another August day glides pointlessly on.
This, you know, is the hour no one likes –
Two to three o'clock. Thoughts grow unfocused.
The afternoon swelters. You wish to sleep
But cannot. In the mid-distance trees sway
In the gentle breeze. Beyond the park gates,
The traffic thins like the cries of children;
A silence, of sorts, listlessly settles.

From the empty municipal buildings
Idle light comes off glass. The minutes

Dawdle along the lashes of your eye;
You hear them singing their monotonous airs
Of mere infinity and nothingness,
Their old unambiguous ironies.

THE SAXOPHONE LESSON

I remember this: once,
The pair of us, lost in silence,
Measuring the unbridgeable gulf
Between each – yourself and myself –

Sensing your pained look, your distress.
No naturalness, tact or finesse.
Like a line cut, nothing passed,
Me, a bookish child to the last,

Simply not having your gift,
Ungainly, self-conscious, stiff,
Fingers like those of a dead man
While yours seemed a well-kept garden,

Elegant, innately fruitful,
Where only the right seemed possible,
Holding each note with dexterous ease,
A glimpse of the small harmonies

I would never know. A clarity,
Bluer, clearer, than the cloudless sky
Where your skill, that bright-plumed bird, took wing,
To leave me alone, floundering,

And always looking up to you,
Imagining your bird's-eye view

Of me – awe-struck, dumbfounded,
Your artless child, ever grounded.

IN FAVOUR OF SPACES

At times, you must walk
to the end of things.

The dusk or the dawn
will always come to cheer you

with unexpected lulls
of silence and cold

where perfections
exist like curios

caught under heavy amber,
cased in frosted glass –

the houses, the roads,
are like willing abandonments,

testaments in a belief
of solitude

and how, even here,
in this city, history

can matter little,
if, indeed, at all . . .

EDAN

Yes, well. What do you want me to say?
It is the coldest night of the year
& yet I lie, unlike you, alone;
my loneliness ringing

like a cry
upon an imaginary landscape
of brown earth & leafless trees,
the prism of white weather.

PAT BORAN
b. 1963

WHEN YOU ARE MOVING INTO A NEW HOUSE

When you are moving into a new house
be slow to write the address in your address books,
because the ghosts who are named there
are constantly seeking new homes,
like fresher students in rain-steamed phone booths.

So by the time you arrive with your books
and frying pan, these ghosts are already
familiar with that easy chair, have found
slow, slow creaks in the floorboards,
are camped on the dream shores of that virgin bed.

CAMDEN STREET IN THE MORNING

Camden Street in the morning, and a man
lifts a piano above his head,
emerging for a day he knows will offer
only rain and criticism:
You eejit, Paddy.
Eight hours of this await him
with reporters asking:
Can she be really worth it?

Even so,
what do they know of his nights,
that tower of pianos silent to the moon?

AMERICAN JUGGLER IN GRAFTON STREET, DUBLIN, OCTOBER 1988

Quiet as Bohr's
celebrated model of the atom,
the balls seem held there
in space and in time
for our scrutiny.

Even the raindrops
are reluctant to fall
before such understanding.

Start young, summarises
an old voice not unwearily.

Perhaps in the laboratory,
with a handful of electrons,
after school is out?

BIOGRAPHY

1 The Choice of Profession

When fish speaks
   the pool records his breath
      on a thin disc
         of water which grows so large
      that it vanishes
   and the utterance is lost
in the stillness

When lion speaks
   the jungle huddles up
      in the background

129

and amplifies the sound
   so it spreads
distorted through the foliage
in the distance

When God speaks
   in the matterlessness
      in the noiselessness
         in the emptiness
      His voice is a clock
   a meter, a calliper
opposite over hypotenuse

Only scientists ever listen

2 Recollections of a Headmaster

'You know, gravity made him cry
when they told him,
and at eighteen he almost
died holding Einstein's
Specific Relativity.

'The *Anatomy Lesson* –
which for most is a piece
of theatre – kept him up nights,
a spectator at his neighbour's
heart bypass.

'Eventually he pronounced
people independent of science,
content to leave discovery,
like power – like the future –
in the hands of a few.

'Seems that microgram of knowledge
weighed like the planet on his shoulders
as though peopled by unthinking giants.'

3 Science Destroys Itself

the Doppler effect of footsteps
$C_8H_{10}N_4O_2$*
& its response
to sugar

the notion
of a space–time continuum
while my watch semaphores
arbitrary hours

the static build-up
on inorganic material
the sector formed by
the eventual door-swing

of your exit
the white hiroshima
of that lone electron
goodbye . . .

*Formula for caffeine

HIS FIRST CONFESSION

Had she come to me with crimes
I'd heard before, or even
crimes unknown (for instance

131

computer fraud – a novelty
yet to reach this parish),
I would gladly have exchanged

the most insignificant
of penances – a running
genuflexion in the aisle . . .

But today the grille and darkness
seemed more for my protection
than presupposed Gothic

decoration. Nine years
old, in finery of First
Confession: *I hate you, Father.*

The stone more silent
than it has ever been,
watching the bright doorway.

FOR A BEEKEEPER

You rise in the morning, the residue
of dream-honey on your eyelids.
Mornings you are not at your best, but then
facing breakfast you remember how
the wings of your bees beat *how many
times a second?* how flowers are identified
by a sense more akin to taste than smell
or sight . . . You see the Queen,
big like a fruit, the precise
network of the honeycomb, the flowers
like excited shopkeepers, opening
their shutters to the sun's gold coin.

There is barely time to shine your shoes
when, already at the window, the first drone
beckons you to court.

A WORD FOR CLOUDS

In her world now six years old
there are common objects yet unnamed,
unfound in the partial vocabularies
of three homes – English,
French, Italian. *Sometimes,*
at night, the moon disappears . . .

The moon disappears behind a white spot
of language. Are we shocked by this
more than by the poverty of love
given her – this child
without clouds in her sky, *sans*
nuages, senza nubi? And
what else besides?

Try telling the young woman
she will become in six years' time:
Every has a silver lining.
The will soon roll by.

WAVE-FUNCTION COLLAPSE IN SEVENTEENTH-CENTURY
   THEATRE

Lear is standing in the margin
describing the closing scene
to the blind Gloucester who
having better hearing than the king

relates the speeches as they happen
with his previously unheard
flair for mimicry

Shakespeare must force himself
to ignore their whisperings
and wind it up

KEVIN SMITH

b. 1963

THE LIGHTNESS OF BEING

It's as if the house has just exploded
And left them standing in a grid of dust –
All their belongings have evaporated,
The new extension somewhere in the stratosphere.
The swelling crowds deduce that sex
Was in the air – it's the middle of the day,
The couple have no clothes on, they look flushed.
The woman's arms are full of breasts
And pubic hair alternately – she feels
Dizzy, as if the world was never really real.
Embarrassment threatens to blow her away.
And the man, her lover, wild-haired, bewildered,
Is holding his penis tightly, as a child would
Clutch the string of a crucial red balloon.

THE JAZZ

How can anyone sleep with all this noise?
The moon balancing over the roof tops
Like a note impossibly sustained,
Cats tuning up for love in Q-sharp,
Gunfire in the hills, those galloping feet . . .

The woman whose eyes haunt the stairs
Is striving for orgasm in the room above,
Her pitch intensifying as the rhythm quickens:
It is a song of fire and ice, tigers and lambs,
Fragmented names called into the dark –

A flock of birds rises out of nowhere.

A SENSE OF PLACE

The pattern forms again, a tattoo of light
On your skin, the chance refraction
Of sun through a fault in the glass,
A watermark signifying nothing more
Than a place, years from now, a door
Into a room, in a city perhaps, the vibrato
Of traffic in a square, the operatics
Of newspaper vendors, a jet soaring into noon –
Where sunlight stands about in hexagons
And rhomboids, dust-mosaics on bare boards.
There is, in your dreams, the perfect room,
A place, it seems, you have always known . . .
This could be it now – the bare boards,
The sun making patterns on your skin.

FROM HEAVEN

Through depths of blue shadow it was falling
Between buildings into the well of the yard,
Bin lids and windowsills rising up
Like slow bread, so soft and luminous

It felt as though we too were falling
Through the dizzy spaces of the afternoon,
Vertiginous moments drifting into hours
That could no more hold than the snow

Already melting on the tongues of roof tops.

PRIMORDIAL

Drowsed by the steam, you half close your eyes
And dream of mud flats and bubbling oceans.
Creatures, croaking songs of evolution,
Crawl towards you from the potential of slime,
Waving half-formed limbs at the future . . .

With the soap you dissolve your hard-earned dirt,
And make a soup of flesh and salt
Which the ravenous mouth will suck away –
Through shining entrails of new technology . . .
Little by little, you return to the sea.

BASEMENT

The strange perfume of an eastern bazaar
Disturbs the senses in a sleazy lunchtime bar.
On one side, four negroes slump against a wall
In attitudes of surly exile. Their unflinching
Silence seems to suck the noise from the air
Of clinking glasses and the moan of the faded jukebox.
With ritual precision, the cylinder
Of smoke is moved from hand to hand,
And from hand to mouth – its weaved circle
A languid choreography of chains.
'Drugs,' the barman is complaining, 'bloody Blacks . . .'
And he turns to draw gold from an optic.
One man, sensing my gaze, lifts his glazed eyes to mine –
Between the whites, the drift of distant sky, sunshine.

MARTIN MOONEY

b. 1964

BUILDING AN ISLAND

The art of playing god has come down in the world –
yesterday these men were boys
being taught the rudiments of the pre-Copernican
universe, its spheres and epicycles
and its hidden engines. Today
they are driving bulldozers and dump trucks
at the edge of a shrinking sea,
they work in a hurricane of gulls,
building an island.

Underneath them, layers of stone
quarried from the demolition sites of the world,
abandoned hospitals, offices
left empty by an exodus of secretaries,
schools whose students have gone
on the children's crusade
into one or other of the forbidden zones.
Underneath that, in turn, the bones
of sea fish fossilise.

After their long migration from the mainland
lifeforms tense and breed.
Evolving new strains, adapting to circumstance,
they will learn to graze
these miraculous flatlands.
Tomorrow the building of houses begins,
already a kind of grass grows on the surface
between the tin cans and oil drums
leaking slime.

LIBERTÉ, ÉGALITÉ, FRATERNITÉ: JOHANNESBURG 1989

It was a summer, the records say, of heat waves,
parched England's moonscaped fields
shimmering under the hole in the ozone layer;
and it was the summer of that thing in China,
anger and optimism, delight, massacre,
all of it, with hindsight, so predictable.
On a more personal note, I've spent
this afternoon going through the notebooks
of my great-grandfather Louis de Klerk,
the Franco-Afrikaner astronomer. Here
is the entry for July fourteenth:

These weeks are too busy with sport
for anyone to notice our small celebrations,
Georges, Philippe, Antoinette and myself
dressed in period costumes, drinking wine
and speechifying on the lawn outside
the Witwatersrand University. The smell
of tear gas might have been bad enough,
and the rival meetings of the student radicals
threatened to get us all arrested,
but the cheer that greeted every cricket score
as England thundered to a great defeat
meant that I could hardly hear myself recite.
I, of course, played Danton. Philippe,
that broad, impatient mind, was Robespierre;
Georges was King and a host of commoners
and bayed for his own head on a platter
with great aplomb. And Antoinette –
poor, sick, beautiful Antoinette, cancer
already killing off the red cells
so that she tired easily and had to go home
after an hour in the sun – what else
should she be but the doomed Queen?

Those too-familiar phrases of Macaulay
returned with a vivid poignancy . . .

He goes on, nothing much of interest:
the newspaper headlines, the rand,
the price of gold on the world markets,
a paragraph on a new discovery
in the constellation of Ursa Minor:
The light that reaches from the dying star
has taken centuries of centuries to get here,
and has left nothing but ash behind it . . .
And then, down in the margin, a scribbled
note from the days of the revolution,
addressed in hope to some historian
of the pre-democratic era, like myself:
Today they have executed Philippe –
Georges and I are in hiding – no one
is safe – two hundred this week –
the hint of a quasar in Andromeda . . .

Three weeks later he went into exile
and died with his ear to a radio telescope,
straining to catch the faintest of signals.

THE SALMON OF KNOWLEDGE

Like anything else, this can be explained:
somewhere over the Atlantic
they are sucked up into a columnar wind
and flung head over tail until
they lose momentum, fall as rain.

Big enough, some of them, to dislodge
slates and guttering, to knock

the chimneypot from the chimney
and kill infants in pushchairs.
One of them, big as a baby, crashed
through our roof and into the cistern
and lived to tell the tale . . .

I had heard of such things – hailstones
the size of footballs, rainstorms
of frogs – but our downpour
was extraordinary all the same.
Nothing as strange has happened here
since the day a century ago
when John Henry Thornton married
his cousin from the mountains.

Now their great-grandchildren
come out-of-doors to look
at the streets full of half-dead fish –
a heliograph of blue and silver –
as if at newly fallen snow,
their eyes wide with astonishment,
their mouths open as if to say,

After this nothing will ever surprise us.
We have seen everything now.

MEN BATHING

after Edvard Munch

Their wet heads are jaggy as pine cones
opening to sunlight on the sill
of the brightest room of the house;
the surf's coarse marbling
is the work of an apprentice painter

learning to woodgrain doors,
a trial-piece in trompe l'oeil
that deceives no one.

Shin-deep,
they are wading out of the sun
as if out of a factory,
each neat, chilled penis cradled
in a nest of wet pubes
like the shell in the *Birth of Venus*.

NOT LOVING IRENE ADLER

As a lover, he would have placed himself in a false
position . . . To admit such intrusions into his own delicate and
finely adjusted temperament was to introduce a distracting
factor which might throw a doubt upon all his mental results.
                              Arthur Conan Doyle, 'A scandal in Bohemia'

Tonight I inhale
Bach violin concertos,
indoor gunfire,
the newly electrified
city streets,
fine porcelain, bonemeal –
all grist to my mill.

A frenzy of high notes
climbs the stairs
to an insomniac
crescendo. A month's
uneaten meals
are a penicillin farm.
I have snow in my face.

' . . . Whatever is left,
however improbable,
must be the truth.'
I was never myself
when we met,
absorbed like sugar
in damp lanes,

my head full of secrets
and empires,
the chill mathematics
of suicide chess
and corruption.
I was a connoisseur,
a skeleton

in a long overcoat,
and felt you
when I worked late,
a shadowboxer
ducking my punches,
a deep-water shoal
always escaping my nets.

'To be left till called for . . . '
The thought of you
is gas lamps in thick fog,
aurora borealis.
At the open window
the night sky is lobster
and turquoise

like a foreign postmark.
Your photograph
collects a fur of ice
in a locked drawer.

Like everything else
in the world, my eyes
are freezing over.

GEORGE GROSZ

This man is a bone stuck in the world's throat.
His tuxedo is festooned with cigars.
His girlfriend is as thin as a fish-hook.

This man is little more than a torso and a head.
His eyes dress always in bandages.
His sons and daughters are derelict houses.

This man believes in electricity and scalpels,
crutches, gramophones, venereal disease . . .
His fists are full of hypodermic needles.

JOHN KELLY

b. 1965

THE LENIN MAUSOLEUM

Were this the clean, green morgue
of the Erne Hospital, at home,
or a prayerful candled bedroom
in a curtained council house,
I'd touch his head and bless myself
and hope he was in heaven.

I'd shake hands with the family
and wait with solemn men
in a hallway he'd papered just
the week before – hard on the wife,
looks well, doesn't he? That week
in Bundoran done him the world of good . . .

In Moscow I pass on through, respectfully,
checking the hands for Rosary beads,
alert in case he moves. And out
the back I offer my condolences
with the only words I know –
Vodka. Glasnost. Kalashnikov.

FIRST WORD

for my mother

There was some crack in our house
when my first word was born –
there was me a matter of months –

mad with a blanket, all slabber
and bib. Raving love and hunger
on the floor.

And the state of the two of you
when I kicked my heels
and out it came so easy.
Big and healthy – as if from
nowhere. My first word –
Czechoslovakia.

But was it any wonder,
with that saint I was never sure about
standing sentry on the sill?
The Child of Prague whispering in my ear
all the holy water night –
Say it, John! Say it!
Czech - os - lo - vak - ya!
Czech - os - lo - vak - ya!

ONE FINE DAY

The Cyrillic clears –
my eyes focus on *Puccini*
and *Cio-Cio-San*
and I know I'm in the right place –
the Leningrad Conservatoire,
the Moldavian State Opera's production
of *Madame Butterfly*.

I've checked up on etiquette –
left my coat in the cloakroom,
I'm casually dressed in open-necked shirt
and determined not to laugh

when she kills herself.
(And I'm quite looking forward to yelling
Bravo! in the accelerando hand clap
at the end.)

In the reading rooms
   a solemn McKeown takes aim
   like a sniper.
   A black ball finish –
   a fine cut to the centre pocket –
   One fine day, he assures himself,
   One fine day . . . from *Madame Butterfly!*

ROME

They tried to rob me
on the Spanish Steps
but I chased then
with an Irish mouthful
and scattered them
like marbles
into swarms of Japanese

and victorious,
I bought *gelato*
in a backstreet
and circled
like a half-mad pigeon,
counting lire
in my head.

FLUNTERN CEMETERY, ZURICH

There is no cross
to make me think of heaven,
just himself, cross-legged
with open book,
remembering,
plotting street names in his head –
listening to the lions' roar
beyond the trees.

AMSTERDAM

I

I hacked off my ear
in the Van Gogh Museum
and slipped it to you,
secretly, in the sunflowers.

And then all bandaged up
I ran like mad through
hissing streets –
hashish!

II

and in my room,
perspective gone,
I was the man
responsible

for every low-cut drunk's
sweet breath
and every fresh-faced
spotted dress,

148

condemned in thought
and word and deed
to wheel a child's
confusing streets,

III

so I hung myself
from a windmill blade,
plumb to the ground
with every revolution.

My neck and hair
were bloody –
those sordid scenes were mine
and I had brought you here.

RIVER

Afraid of my life
I'll see what's down there,
I just thank God
there's no glass bottom
in my boat,
for true as God
this water should be red
where every drop
is one man dead
and every whirlpool
the spiracle of a soul.
And beyond the bridge
the water widens
and currents claw
in desperate little waltzes
to themselves,

creasing, spiralling, sucking –
the crawling skin of river,
poisonous in my wake,
the weightless tangle
of a dead swan.

THE DAY WILLIAM BUTLER YEATS WAS ON THE BUS

William Butler Yeats
sat beside me
on the Enniskillen bus;

listening to a personal stereo,
hands clamped to his ears,
he caught me looking at him
and he leaned over –
his nose went the whole way down his face –
Yeah! he said, *Rave on! Rave on!*
He pointed at his ears
and closed his eyes –
Van Morrison! he whispered,
Van Morrison!
I'm a great man for Van the Man so I am!
I didn't know what to say
and everyone was looking round –
he doesn't be on the bus that often.
Ah I'm a great man for Van the Man!
he said (automatically).
I'm starting a band, you know!
I'm thinking of calling it
Krazy Jane and the Kool Swans.
Kool with a K.
The first single's called
Byzantium in a Jamjar.

He opened his jacket with grace –
a T-shirt – a picture of him
and the *Tread Softly World Tour '77*
written across it –
Ah I'm a great man for Van the Man so I am!
Georgie Fame!
And he seemed to drift away.

It was sad that night in The Vintage –
Yeats was the cabaret,
himself, a guitar and a drum machine –
Here Comes the Knight
Into the Mystic
and one he said he'd written himself –
a desperate waltztime version
of *The Sally Gardens*.

SARA BERKELEY

b. 1967

I AM LYING WHERE I'VE FALLEN

I am lying where I've fallen
And I am not proud
Of night swinging crazily to and fro,
For the sands are swallowing over my head
And I know the hidden rock.

Straight as the stone is cut
The shadow falls
And you, in an ugly mood,
Say the soul must know what it is looking for
And carry me under one arm, roots dangling.

Yours is that hard mercy –
Blood and bones and spirit of mine
Kicked in the womb against living,
And kick all my life against
So many different things that could be my death.

We go back and we come forwards
In the bitter knowledge of perfection,
The pendulum of spent rage
Hung still when I left your circle
And the flesh healed as though I had never been.

I still lie where I have fallen
In the dust and clay where you've been
Running rings around a mountain foot.
Looking just the same
You come
Oh you
You
You.

DEATH IN A STRANGER'S HEAD

Four years since you
Laid your hand on the wicker gate,
Coming with a half-child's face
As close as you dared,
Looking to me for reason
Having died in a lover's head somewhere.

And I –
I saw a running light and describing it, said,
It is love without beginning or end,
It is the tightest circle round the sun
And you will thrive in the memory of no one.

But having died in a stranger's head
You were looking for the moist earth,
The silence of burial,
And it was not reason
Saying here was a man, coming
Unbound to a nub of pain
From a lover's unopened door
Nor was it reason
Dictating that you should come to me for more
Of this troubled shame.

Four years since the night
I slept, while you were torn apart
Questioning whether the elements really were
Air, fire, water, love, earth.

And when you came wearily to my bed
I felt that you were hot to the bare soles
And later I heard you in your sleep,
You said no, no.

WE GET ALONG

We get along like two
Houses on fire. We burn excitedly,
Swopping flames, crackling with joy –
Let it always be so,
Oh let it always.

I'm tired of going round and round,
My tail in my mouth;
Every revolution makes me fear
I've always been wrong
About everything; but we get along
Like two houses alight
And spitting stars, our laughter
Is less of a secret,
More of a shout
Into the endless, flame-shot
Night.

HOME-MOVIE NIGHTS

Ratcheted, in stills,
How thin and brown the smooth-limbed
Brothers, throwing off their casts of sand
(Bury me! I am a dead man!),
Framed in loose rolls of celluloid
And I, smaller even than the buried ones
Up there on our sitting-room wall.
I was once caught under a giant wave.
They brought me out alive
(They did not save my life
For I was saved on celluloid)
But through the wave I saw them dive for me.

154

All my life they brought me, pearl-like, from the waves
And now, well used to handling the names
Of men long gone from me and unfamiliar grown
And opening the letters home
I do most of my
Wringing of hands
Alone.

THE DROWNING ELEMENT

He leans to her with his red liar's hand,
Under the swelling cotton she carries the second child
No longer trusting him –
The small head movements as she sews
Mute assurance that the child grows –
Smiling, and not trusting him at all.

So little beauty to it now,
He treads the eggshell joy
And when it is time for the right word
And he misunderstands, as she had known he would,
She smiles, and lays one hand flat
Over the bruise
Watching it spread like a stain
At the hottest part of the day;
Coming up for air
To a place where there is always water,
Surfacing to a black place,
That colour flocking to her hair,
Her eyes, the clothes she wears.

Returning late, he pours the dregs of his day
Into her lap
Until he has spilled out every drop,

She shakes it out into the dying fire
And meets the dark of the bedroom with her own dark
Aware he is blind to the drowning element in things,
Minnowing down through a pool of sleep
To a deep rest on the rock bed.

WINTERING

Of course I feel you gathering up to leave.
In our tightest, briefest arguments
I crush nettles with my blind left hand,
The child in me peers through a grid of fingers,
My eyes are an open wound.

Your lies have piranha teeth
Freshwater white,
The stones of the river grieve
Until they are worn smooth,
And pain has its way with me –
A great fish, nosing at my spine.

Because I will not try to blunt
This helpless, piercing sight
You push me to one side,
The cold air salts my face,
Perhaps this, too, is a cure,
For you are slight
And leave no trace.
My hand digests the slowest nettle juice,
I have no scars to show
But I have heard
The muttered refrain of wintering
Tremble up from a flurry of dried leaves
At your heel; it goes –
Bury me, I shall grow in spring.

BIOGRAPHICAL AND
BIBLIOGRAPHICAL NOTES

SEBASTIAN BARRY

b. 1955 in Dublin. Educated at the Catholic University School and Trinity College Dublin. He has written extensively as a poet, playwright and novelist.

PUBLICATIONS

Poetry
The Water-Colourist, Dolmen Press, 1983
The Rhetorical Town, Dolmen Press, 1985
Fanny Hawke Goes to the Mainland Forever, Raven Arts Press, 1989
Fiction
Macker's Garden, Co-op Books, 1982
Time out of Mind – Strappado Square, Wolfhound Press, 1983
The Engine of Owl-Light, Paladin, 1987
Drama
Boss Grady's Boys, Raven Arts Press, 1989

SARA BERKELEY

b. 1967 in Dublin. Educated at Trinity College Dublin and the University of California at Berkeley. Currently living in London.

PUBLICATIONS

Poetry
Penn, Raven Arts Press, 1986
Home-Movie Nights, Raven Arts Press, 1989

DERMOT BOLGER

b. 1959 in Dublin. Co-founder of Raven Arts Press, he has received several awards for his work as poet, novelist and publisher. He has also written plays.

PUBLICATIONS

Poetry
The Habit of Flesh, Raven Arts Press, 1980
Finglas Lilies, Raven Arts Press, 1981
No Waiting America, Raven Arts Press, 1982
Internal Exiles, Dolmen Press, 1986
Leinster Street Ghosts, Raven Arts Press, 1989

Fiction
Night Shift, Brandon, 1985
The Woman's Daughter, Raven Arts Press, 1987; revised edition,
 Viking, 1991
The Journey Home, Penguin/Viking, 1990

PAT BORAN

b. 1963 in Portlaoise. He has written short stories and radio plays
as well as poetry. Now lives in Dublin where he has worked as an
administrator of Poetry Ireland.

PUBLICATIONS

Poetry
The Unwound Clock, Dedalus Press, 1990
History and Promise: Poems from Laois, International University
 Press, 1990

MAIRÉAD BYRNE

b. 1957 in Dublin. After a degree in English Language and Literature
and some postgraduate work at University College Dublin, she
worked as a freelance journalist and broadcaster for a period of ten
years. She is now director of the Belltable Arts Centre in Limerick.

BRENDAN CLEARY

b. 1958 in County Antrim. Presently lives in Newcastle upon Tyne
where he works as a part-time lecturer and performance poet. Editor
of the *Echo Room* poetry magazine, he has published several pamph-
lets of poetry.

SEÁN DUNNE

b. 1956 in Waterford. Now lives in Cork where he works as a
journalist on the *Cork Examiner*. He has contributed poems, articles
and reviews to many magazines and journals in Ireland, Britain and
the United States.

PUBLICATIONS
Poetry
Against the Storm, Dolmen Press, 1986
Poets of Munster (ed.), Brandon/Anvil, 1986

ANDREW ELLIOTT
b. 1961 in Limavady, County Derry. Educated at Queen's University Belfast. His poetry featured in *Trio Poetry 4* (Blackstaff Press, 1985). In 1985 he was the first recipient of the Allan Dowling Poetry Travelling Fellowship, which he used for a year's visit to the USA. Currently lives in London.

PUBLICATIONS
Poetry
The Creationists, Blackstaff Press, 1988

RITA ANN HIGGINS
b. 1955 in Galway. Was writer-in-residence at the Galway City Library. She has given many readings of her work in Ireland and Britain.

PUBLICATIONS
Poetry
Goddess on the Mervue Bus, Salmon Press, 1986
Witch in the Bushes, Salmon Press, 1988
Goddess and Witch, Salmon Press, 1990

JOHN HUGHES
b. 1962 in Belfast. Educated at St Patrick's High School, Downpatrick, and Queen's University Belfast. Has lived in New York, and is currently based in Belfast.

PUBLICATIONS
Poetry
The Something in Particular, Gallery Press, 1986

JOHN KELLY

b. 1965 in Enniskillen, County Fermanagh. Graduated in Law from Queen's University Belfast. Currently works as a broadcaster for the BBC. His poems have been published and broadcast widely in Ireland and Britain, and in 1990 he did a reading tour in the USA.

THOMAS MCCARTHY

b. 1954 in County Waterford. Educated at University College Cork. He works in the Cork City Library and has received several awards, including the American-Irish Foundation's Literary Award for 1984.

PUBLICATIONS

Poetry
The First Convention, Dolmen Press, 1978
The Sorrow Garden, Anvil Press, 1981
The Non-Aligned Storyteller, Anvil Press, 1984
Seven Winters in Paris, Dedalus Press/Anvil Press, 1989

PETER MCDONALD

b. 1962 in Belfast. Educated at Methodist College Belfast and University College, Oxford. He is now a fellow and lecturer in English at Pembroke College, Cambridge.

PUBLICATIONS

Poetry
Biting the Wax, Bloodaxe Books, 1989

Criticism
Louis MacNeice: The Poet in his Contexts, Oxford University Press, 1990

AIDAN CARL MATHEWS

b. 1956 in Dublin. Educated at Gonzaga College, University College Dublin, Trinity College Dublin and Stanford University in California. Currently a producer with RTE radio drama. He has won several awards for his poetry and fiction and is also well known as a playwright.

PUBLICATIONS

Poetry
Windfalls, Dolmen Press, 1976
Minding Ruth, Gallery Press, 1983

Fiction
Adventures in a Bathyscope, Secker and Warburg, 1988
Muesli at Midnight, Secker and Warburg, 1990

Drama
Exit/Entrance, Gallery Press, 1990

MARTIN MOONEY

b. 1964 in Belfast. Studied at Queen's University Belfast and has published poetry in *Trio Poetry 5* (Blackstaff Press, 1987) and in various magazines in Ireland, Britain and elsewhere. Co-editor of *Map-Makers' Colours* and *Rhinoceros* poetry magazine.

JULIE O'CALLAGHAN

b. 1954 in Chicago. Has lived in Ireland since 1974 and works as a librarian in Dublin. Her poems have appeared widely in Ireland, Britain and the United States. She has also written poetry for children.

PUBLICATIONS

Poetry
Edible Anecdotes, Dolmen Press, 1983 (Poetry Book Society
   Recommendation)
What's What, Bloodaxe Books, 1991

Children's poetry
Taking My Pen for a Walk, Collins, 1990

DENNIS O'DRISCOLL

b. 1954 in Thurles, County Tipperary. His poems and reviews have been published extensively in Ireland and Britain. A civil servant since 1970, he works in Dublin Castle.

PUBLICATIONS

Poetry
Kist, Dolmen Press, 1982
Hidden Extras, Dedalus Press/Anvil Press, 1987

MICHAEL O'LOUGHLIN

b. 1958 in Dublin. Has spent some years in Barcelona and now lives in Amsterdam.

PUBLICATIONS

Poetry
Stalingrad: The Street Dictionary, Raven Arts Press, 1980
Atlantic Blues, Raven Arts Press, 1982
The Diary of a Silence, Raven Arts Press, 1985

Fiction
The Inside Story, Raven Arts Press, 1989

Translation
Hidden Weddings: Selected Poems of Gerrit Achterberg, Raven Arts
    Press, 1987

Criticism
Patrick Kavanagh and the Discourse of Contemporary Irish Poetry,
    Raven Arts Press, 1985

PATRICK RAMSEY

b. 1962 in New Jersey, USA. Has lived in Belfast since 1970 when his family returned to Northern Ireland. A graduate of Queen's University Belfast, he currently works for *Fortnight* in Belfast. His poems have appeared in various magazines and in *Trio Poetry 6* (Blackstaff Press, 1990). He co-edits *Rhinoceros* and is founder-editor of Lagan Press, an independent publishing house in Belfast.

PETER SIRR

b. 1960 in Waterford. Educated at Trinity College Dublin. He is one of the editors of *Graph* and has lived and worked in Holland and Italy.

PUBLICATIONS

Poetry
Marginal Zones, Gallery Press, 1984
Talk, Talk, Gallery Press, 1987

KEVIN SMITH

b. 1963 in London. A graduate of Queen's University Belfast, he works as a journalist in Belfast. He has edited the *Gown Literary Supplement*, and has been literary editor of the *Belfast Review* and *Rhinoceros*. His poems have appeared in several literary magazines in Ireland and Britain.

SELECT BIBLIOGRAPHY

GENERAL

Andrews, Elmer (ed.). *Contemporary Irish Poetry: A Collection of Critical Essays*, Macmillan, 1991

Brown, Terence and Nicholas Grene (eds). *Tradition and Influence in Anglo-Irish Poetry*, Macmillan, 1989

Corcoran, Neil (ed.). *The Chosen Ground: Essays on the Contemporary Poetry of Northern Ireland*, Poetry Wales Press/Severn Books, 1991

Dawe, Gerald. *How's the Poetry Going? Literary Politics and Ireland Today*, Lagan Press, 1991

Deane, Seamus. *A Short History of Irish Literature*, Hutchinson, 1986

Kenneally, Michael (ed.). *Cultural Contexts and Literary Idioms*, Colin Smythe, 1989

Longley, Edna. *Poetry in the Wars*, Bloodaxe Books, 1986

Paulin, Tom. *Ireland and the English Crisis*, Bloodaxe Books, 1985

ANTHOLOGIES

Bolger, Dermot. *An Tonn Gheal: The Bright Wave*, Raven Arts Press, 1986

Dawe, Gerald. *The Younger Irish Poets*, Blackstaff Press, 1982

Deane, Seamus (general editor) and Andrew Carpenter (associate editor). *The Field Day Anthology of Irish Writing c. 550–1990*, 3 vols, Field Day, forthcoming, 1991

Fallon, Peter and Derek Mahon. *The Penguin Book of Contemporary Irish Poetry*, Penguin, 1990

Montague, John. *The Faber Book of Irish Verse*, Faber and Faber, 1974

Montague, John. *Bitter Harvest: An Anthology of Contemporary Irish Verse*, Scribner's, 1989

Ormsby, Frank. *Poets from the North of Ireland*, new ed., Blackstaff Press, 1990

Swift, Todd and Martin Mooney. *Map-Makers' Colours: New Poets of Northern Ireland*, Nu-age Editions, 1988

POETRY PUBLISHERS

Beaver Row Press, 9 Beaver Row, Dublin 4
Blackstaff Press, 3 Galway Park, Dundonald, Belfast BT16 0AN
Dedalus Press, 24 The Heath, Cypress Downs, Dublin W6
Gallery Press, Loughcrew, Oldcastle, County Meath
Raven Arts Press, PO Box 1430, Finglas, Dublin 11
Salmon Press, Auburn House, Upper Fairhill, Galway

Cyphers, 3 Selskar Terrace, Ranelagh, Dublin 6
Gown Literary Supplement, Students' Union, Queen's University
  Belfast, Belfast BT7 1NN
Graph, 34 Bellevue Park Avenue, Booterstown, County Dublin
Honest Ulsterman, 159 Lower Braniel Road, Belfast BT5 7NN
Irish Review, University College, Cork
Irish University Review, Department of English, University College,
  Belfield, Dublin 4
Krino, Glenrevagh, Corrandulla, County Galway
Poetry Ireland Review, 44 Upper Mount Street, Dublin 2
Rhinoceros, Flat 3, 90 University Street, Belfast BT7 1HG
Salmon, Auburn House, Upper Fairhill, Galway

ACKNOWLEDGEMENTS

Grateful acknowledgement is made to:

Anvil Press for permission to reprint the following poems by
Thomas McCarthy: 'Returning to de Valera's cottage', 'Her
widowhood' and 'The provincial writer's diary' from *The Sorrow
Garden* (1981); 'The president's men', 'Question time' and
'Windows' from *The Non-Aligned Storyteller* (1984)

Sebastian Barry for permission to reprint the following poems:
'Hermaphroditus' and 'Summer desk' from *The Water-Colourist*
(Dolmen Press, 1983); 'At a gate of St Stephen's Green' from *The
Rhetorical Town* (Dolmen Press, 1985)

Bloodaxe Books for permission to reprint the following poems by
Peter McDonald: 'Short story', 'Unnatural acts' (extract), 'Out of
Ireland', 'Pleasures of the imagination', 'Killers', 'A short history
of the world' and 'The green, grassy slopes of the Boyne' from
Biting the Wax (1989)

Dermot Bolger for permission to reprint the following poems: 'The
man who stepped out of feeling' (extract), 'I am Ireland' and
'Snuff movies' from *Internal Exiles* (Dolmen Press, 1986)

Mairéad Byrne for permission to reprint the following poems: 'An
interview with Romulus and Remus', 'Glory days', 'The
Christmas', 'Post-natal ward', 'Saint Valentine's Day, Kilkenny',
'The new curriculum' and 'Elegy without tooth or heart'

Brendan Cleary for permission to reprint the following poems:
'Born again', 'Scratchmarks', 'Home brew & video', 'Grounds of
asylum', 'More than coffee', 'Devils' and 'Comrades'

Dedalus Press for permission to reprint the following poems by
Pat Boran: 'When you are moving into a new house', 'Camden
Street in the morning', 'American juggler in Grafton Street,
Dublin, October 1988', 'Biography', 'His first confession', 'For a
beekeeper', 'A word for clouds' and 'Wave-function collapse in
seventeenth-century theatre' from *The Unwound Clock* (1990)

Dedalus Press/Anvil Press for permission to reprint the following
poem by Thomas McCarthy: 'The standing trains' from *Seven
Winters in Paris* (1989); for permission to reprint the following
poems by Dennis O'Driscoll: 'Republican sympathies' and 'Home
affairs' from *Hidden Extras* (1987)

Seán Dunne for permission to reprint the following poems: 'Against the storm', 'The fifth Beatle' and 'Quakers' from *Against the Storm* (Dolmen Press, 1986) and 'Marmalade and Mrs Mandlestam', 'Throwing the beads', 'Wittgenstein in Ireland' and 'Letter from Ireland' (extract)

Andrew Elliott for permission to reprint the following poems: 'One of Laura Marx's letters', 'Cleanliness', 'Eavesdropping', Rodin's headache' and 'Peepshow' from *The Creationists* (Blackstaff Press, 1988)

Gallery Press for permission to reprint the following poems by John Hughes: 'Double indemnity', 'Tell-tale', 'A respect for law and order', 'Dada' and 'Puritans and cavaliers' from *The Something in Particular* (1986); for permission to reprint the following poems by Aidan Carl Mathews: 'Letter following', 'Elegy for a five year old', 'For Simon, at three and five', 'The death of Irish', 'Minding Ruth' and 'History notes' from *Minding Ruth* (1983); for permission to reprint the following poems by Peter Sirr: 'Yorick', 'Guido Cavalcanti to his father', 'In the Japanese Garden', 'The collector's marginalia' and 'Landscapes' from *Marginal Zones* (1984); 'Smoke', 'Fly', 'Talk, talk' and 'Vigils' from *Talk, Talk* (1987)

Rita Ann Higgins for permission to reprint the following poems: 'Light of the moon' and 'Limits'

John Hughes for permission to reprint the following poems: 'Flame', 'Cassandra', 'Fairytale doctors', 'Babylon tide' and 'The chill wind'

John Kelly for permission to reprint the following poems: 'The Lenin mausoleum', 'First word', 'One fine day', 'Rome', 'Fluntern cemetery, Zurich', 'Amsterdam', 'River' and 'The day William Butler Yeats was on the bus'

Thomas McCarthy for permission to reprint the following poems: 'State funeral' and 'Breaking garden' from *The First Convention* (Dolmen Press, 1978) and 'Shroud'

Martin Mooney for permission to reprint the following poems: 'Building an island', '*Liberté, égalité, fraternité:* Johannesburg 1989', 'The salmon of knowledge', 'Men bathing', 'Not loving Irene Adler' and 'George Grosz'

Julie O'Callaghan for permission to reprint the following poems: 'Days', 'Three paintings by Edward Hopper', 'The object', 'Tea break', 'The little girl', 'What I saw', 'Marketing' and 'A tourist comments on the land of his forefathers' from *Edible Anecdotes*

169

(Dolmen Press, 1983) and 'Opening lines: twelve dramaticules' (extracts) and 'The Great Blasket Island'

Dennis O'Driscoll for permission to reprint the following poems: 'Flatland', 'Porlock' and 'Wings' from *Kist* (Dolmen Press, 1982) and 'A lament for Willy Loman', 'Remembering Marina Tsvetayeva' and 'The conformist village'

Patrick Ramsey for permission to reprint the following poems: 'Tableau for the New Year', 'Retreat', 'For certain poets', 'Thought at Central Station', 'An afternoon in the park', 'The saxophone lesson', 'In favour of spaces' and 'Edan'

Raven Arts Press for permission to reprint the following poems by Sebastian Barry: 'Fanny Hawke goes to the mainland forever', 'Lines discovered under the foundations of Dublin in a language neither Irish nor English' and 'Trooper O'Hara at the Indian Wars' from *Fanny Hawke Goes to the Mainland Forever* (1989); for permission to reprint the following poems by Sara Berkeley: 'I am lying where I've fallen' and 'Death in a stranger's head' from *Penn* (1986); 'We get along', 'Home-movie nights', 'The drowning element' and 'Wintering' from *Home-Movie Nights* (1989); for permission to reprint the following poems by Dermot Bolger: 'Finglas lilies' (extract) and 'Finglas ballads' (extract) from *Finglas Lilies* (1981); 'Stardust' from *No Waiting America* (1982); 'Halifax, Nova Scotia' from *Leinster Street Ghosts* (1989); for permission to reprint the following poems by Michael O'Loughlin: 'The city' from *Stalingrad: The Street Dictionary* (1980); 'Some old black soul woman' and 'Hamlet in Dublin' from *Atlantic Blues* (1982); 'In the suburbs' (extract), 'The smile', 'Intensity, exaltation', 'Anne Frank' and 'On hearing Michael Hartnett read his poetry in Irish' from *The Diary of a Silence* (1985)

Salmon Press for permission to reprint the following poems by Rita Ann Higgins: 'Secrets' and 'Sunny side plucked' from *Goddess on the Mervue Bus* (1986); 'Some people', 'Witch in the bushes', 'It wasn't the father's fault' and 'Daughter of the Falls Road' from *Witch in the Bushes* (1988)

Kevin Smith for permission to reprint the following poems: 'The lightness of being', 'The jazz', 'A sense of place', 'From heaven', 'Primordial' and 'Basement'

The publishers have made every effort to trace and acknowledge copyright holders. We apologise for any omissions in the above list and we will welcome additions or amendments to it for inclusion in any reprint edition.

INDEX OF FIRST LINES AND TITLES

174